Slow Cookers

Published in 2008 by Murdoch Books Pty Limited
This edition published 2010

Murdoch Books Pty Ltd
Pier 8/9, 23 Hickson Road,
Millers Point NSW 2000
Phone: + 61 (0) 2 8220 2000
Fax: + 61 (0) 2 8220 2558
www.murdochbooks.com.au

Murdoch Books UK Limited
Erico House, 6th Floor
93–99 Upper Richmond Road
Putney, London SW15 2TG
Phone: +44 (0)20 8785 5995
Fax: +44 (0)20 8785 5985
www.murdochbooks.co.uk

Chief Executive: Juliet Rogers
Publishing Director: Kay Scarlett

Publisher: Lynn Lewis
Design concept and illustrations: Heather Menzies
Designer: Clare O'Loughlin
Editor: Kim Rowney
Food Editor: Alison Adams
Production: Joan Beal
Editorial Coordinator: Liz Malcolm
Recipes developed by Alison Adams, Peta Dent, Michelle Earl, Vicky Harris and the
Murdoch Books Test Kitchen

National Library of Australia Cataloguing-in-Publication Data
Title: Slow Cookers. Includes index.
ISBN 9781741968958 (pbk.)
Subjects: Electronic cookery, slow. Casserole cookery.
Dewey number: 641.5884

PRINTED IN CHINA

IMPORTANT: Those who might be at risk from the effects of salmonella poisoning (the elderly, pregnant women, young children and
those suffering from immune deficiency diseases) should consult their doctor with any concerns about eating raw eggs.

CONVERSION GUIDE: You may find cooking times vary depending on the oven you are using.
For fan-forced ovens, as a general rule, set the oven temperature to 20°C (35°F) lower than indicated in the recipe.

Slow Cookers

more than 100 easy recipes

MURDOCH BOOKS

Contents

Hearty family fare

Trends come and go, and when it comes to kitchen gadgetry, we've possibly seen them all. From omelette makers, ice-cream machines and bread makers to plug-in tagines and electric tin openers, it seems there's been an electrical appliance invented for every culinary situation imaginable. Yet how many of us have succumbed to the latest, greatest gizmo, only to discover that it takes up too much space in our cupboards or is annoyingly hard to clean? Having said that, there are some machines and appliances we'd rather not live without. Food processors, blenders and electric beaters have removed a great deal of tedious elbow grease from much of our cooking and we'd be hard pressed to cook successfully without them. Slow cookers are another indispensable kitchen device that no busy household should be without. They've been around since the 1960s and have always had their devotees, but more and more cooks are wising up to the time- and budget-saving capabilities of the slow cooker.

Slow cookers transform many foods (particularly those tougher, tastier cuts of meat) from their raw state to melting tenderness, with not much more exertion than flicking a switch. They can be plugged in anywhere, they use less electricity than your oven, and there is only one bowl to wash up afterwards. You don't need to stir or hover over a meal simmering in a slow cooker and it's almost impossible to burn anything; there's such latitude in cooking times that an hour or two more isn't going to make much difference. In a slow cooker, meals practically cook themselves and they taste incredible — every last drop of the food's natural flavour is captured inside the cooker.

From hearty soups such as seafood chowder and pea and ham soup to creamy chicken curry, country beef stew and lamb shanks in red wine, the hardest thing about using your slow cooker will be deciding what to make in it.Slow cookers are also called 'Crock Pots'; Crock Pot is a brand name that was conjured up in America in 1971. Essentially, a slow cooker is an electrical appliance, comprising a round, oval or oblong cooking vessel made of glazed ceramic or porcelain. This is surrounded by a metal housing, which contains a thermostatically controlled element. The lid, which is often transparent, makes it easy to check the progress of what's cooking inside. The recipes in this book were developed using a 4.5 litre (157 fl oz/18 cup) slow cooker but they come in a variety of sizes, with the largest having a capacity of around 7 litres (245 fl oz/28 cups). Note that slow cookers work best when they are at least half, and preferably three-quarters, full (the operating manual that comes with your model will advise you on this).

Most models of slow cookers have a number of temperature settings and typically these are 'low', 'medium' and 'high'. The 'low' setting cooks foods at around 80°C (175°F) while 'high' cooks foods at around 90°C (195°F). 'Medium' is a combination of these two temperatures; when set to medium the slow cooker cooks for around an hour at 'high', then automatically clicks to 'low' and continues cooking at that temperature. As a general rule, cooking on 'low' doubles the cooking time from a 'high' setting and you can tweak the cooking times of recipes to longer or shorter. Recipe cooking times vary from 3 to 12 hours.

At its simplest, to use your slow cooker all you need to do is prepare and chop your ingredients, add liquid (water, wine or stock) and turn it on, leaving the contents to murmur away until cooked to lush tenderness. Time-strapped cooks can put ingredients in the slow cooker before work and return home at night to a dinner ready-to-go; or, meals can be cooked overnight. The cooking environment in a slow cooker is very moist, making it perfect for tough cuts of meat such as beef blade, lamb or veal shanks, or pork belly. Such cuts contain a great quantity of connective tissues and these can only be broken down with long, slow cooking. When preparing meat, it is important that you trim fatty meat well, as the fat tends to settle on top of the juices.

The slow cooker requires less liquid than normal stovetop or oven cookery, as there is no chance for the liquid to evaporate. In fact, many foods, including some meats, release moisture of their own during cooking (up to one cup per average recipe), so bear this in mind when you think a recipe doesn't have enough liquid in it, or when adapting recipes for the slow cooker (when adapting standard recipes for the slow cooker cut the liquid by 50 per cent). Resist the urge to lift the lid during cooking, particularly at the beginning, as the slow cooker takes a while to heat up, and always cook with the lid on unless the recipe instructs otherwise — perhaps when thickening a sauce. If you need to remove the lid to stir or to check the food is cooked, replace the lid quickly so the slow cooker doesn't lose too much heat.

It is difficult to overcook tougher meats but it is possible (the meat will turn raggedy and fall apart into thin shreds) so you still need to use the suggested cooking times for each recipe. Keep in mind, however, that cooking times may vary, depending on the brand and size of slow cooker you are using. And, because cooking times are fairly approximate, we have rounded our cooking times to the nearest 15 minutes.

While most recipes use the slow cooker as a true one-pot solution, where everything goes in together at the start, other recipes use the cooker as the primary mode of cooking but use other steps along the way. Optionally you can brown meats such as pork, beef or lamb on the stovetop first, before adding them to the cooker. Meat gains extra flavour when browned, as the outside surfaces caramelise over high temperatures (about 100°C/210°F) and this cannot be achieved in a slow cooker. Recipes in the entertaining chapter of this book include this extra step but for any meat recipe, you can choose to brown first if you like.

Hard vegetables such as root vegetables can take a very long time to cook, so cut them into smallish pieces and push them to the base of the cooker or around the side, where the heat is slightly greater. Green vegetables can lose some nutrients if cooked for prolonged periods, so blanch them first (if required) and add them at the end of cooking to heat through. Seafood and dairy products should also be added to the slow cooker near the end of cooking.

Food safety

In the past there have been concerns about food safety issues with slow cookers, namely whether harmful bacteria that are present in foods, particularly in meats, are killed at such low temperatures. However, bacteria are killed off at around 68°C (155°F), so users of slow cookers need not be concerned about bacteria. One rule here though is to never place meats that are still frozen, or partially frozen, in a slow cooker as this scenario can cause food–poisoning bacteria to flourish; ALWAYS have meats thawed fully before cooking. And never use the ceramic insert after it has been frozen or refrigerated as the sudden change in temperature could cause it to crack.

Another caveat is that you cannot cook dried red kidney beans from their raw state in the slow cooker because the temperature is not high enough to destroy the natural toxins found in these beans. Dried red kidney beans, and other dried beans, need to be boiled for 10 minutes to destroy these toxins. Tinned beans however are safe for immediate use. To prepare dried beans, soak the beans in water for 5 hours or overnight. Discard the water, then rapidly boil the beans in fresh water for 10 minutes to destroy the toxins.

* Make sure you read the manufacturer's instructions for the safe use of your slow cooker.

Soups

A meal in a bowl is a very
comforting prospect at the end of a busy
day. Just add bread or a salad.

FRENCH ONION SOUP

preparation time 20 minutes
cooking time 6 hours
serves 4

20 g (³/4 oz) butter
1 tablespoon olive oil
1 kg (2 lb 4 oz) brown onions,
   thinly sliced
250 ml (9 fl oz/1 cup) dry white wine

2 tablespoons brandy (optional)
750 ml (26 fl oz/3 cups) beef stock
4 thyme sprigs
2 tablespoons finely chopped
   flat-leaf (Italian) parsley

• Put the butter, olive oil and onion in the slow cooker. Cook on low for 4 hours, stirring occasionally.

• Add wine, brandy (if using), stock, 250 ml (9 fl oz/1 cup) water and thyme. Cook on high for a further 2 hours. Season to taste with salt and freshly ground black pepper. Sprinkle with the parsley and serve with crusty bread.

POTATO AND LEEK SOUP

preparation time 10 minutes
cooking time 3 hours
serves 4

4 all-purpose potatoes, roughly
   chopped
2 leeks, white part only, thinly sliced
2 celery stalks, chopped
1 carrot, chopped

2 prosciutto slices, roughly chopped
500 ml (17 fl oz/2 cups) chicken or
   vegetable stock
pouring cream, to serve

● Put the potato, leek, celery, carrot, prosciutto, stock and 500 ml
(17 fl oz/2 cups) water in the slow cooker. Cook on high for 3 hours.

● Using a hand-held stick blender, purée the soup until smooth. Alternatively,
transfer the soup mixture to a food processor and purée until smooth. Season
to taste with salt and freshly ground black pepper. Ladle the soup into bowls
and serve drizzled with cream.

CREAM OF MUSHROOM SOUP

preparation time 20 minutes +
cooking time 2 hours
serves 4

10 g ($^1/_4$ oz) dried porcini mushrooms
1 leek, white part only, thinly sliced
100 g ($3^1/_2$ oz) pancetta or bacon,
   chopped 200 g (7 oz) Swiss brown
   mushrooms, roughly chopped
300 g ($10^1/_2$ oz) large field
   mushrooms, roughly chopped
125 ml (4 fl oz/$^1/_2$ cup) Madeira
   (Malmsey) (see Note)

1 litre (35 fl oz/4 cups) chicken or
   vegetable stock
2 teaspoons chopped marjoram
90 g ($3^1/_4$ oz/$^1/_3$ cup) light sour cream
   or crème fraîche
marjoram leaves, extra, to garnish

• Soak the porcini in 250 ml (9 fl oz/1 cup) boiling water for 20 minutes. Drain, reserving the soaking water.

• Combine the porcini and the soaking water, leek, pancetta or bacon, swiss brown and field mushrooms, madeira, stock and half of the chopped marjoram in the slow cooker. Cook on high for 2 hours.

• Using a hand-held stick blender, purée the soup. Alternatively, transfer the soup mixture to a food processor and purée until smooth, then return the soup to the slow cooker.

• Stir through sour cream and cook for a further 5 minutes, then stir through the remaining chopped marjoram. Garnish with marjoram leaves and serve with crusty bread.

note *Madeira is a fortified wine made in Portugal. Malmsey is the richest and fruitiest of the Madeiras and it can also be drunk as an after-dinner drink. If unavailable, use sherry.*

VEGETABLE AND CHEDDAR SOUP

preparation time 15 minutes
cooking time 3–4 hours
serves 4

2 all-purpose potatoes
   (about 250 g/9 oz), diced
2 zucchini (courgettes), diced
1 carrot, diced
1 celery stalk, diced
3 spring onions (scallions),
   finely chopped

1 litre (35 fl oz/4 cups) chicken
   or vegetable stock
425 g (15 oz) tinned creamed corn
125 g (4$^{1}/_2$ oz/1 cup) grated
   cheddar cheese
2 tablespoons finely chopped
   flat-leaf (Italian) parsley

● Put the potato, zucchini, carrot, celery and spring onion in slow cooker.
Add stock and season well with salt and freshly ground black pepper. Cook
on high for 3–4 hours, or until the vegetables are cooked.

● Just before serving, stir in the creamed corn, cheese and parsley. Season
to taste with salt and pepper. Serve when the cheese has just melted and
the soup has heated through.

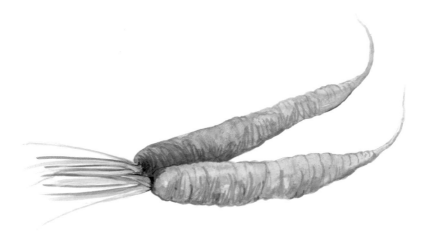

BUTTERNUT PUMPKIN SOUP

preparation time 15 minutes
cooking time 3 hours
serves 4

1.25 kg (2 lb 12 oz) butternut
  pumpkin (squash), peeled, seeded
  and chopped into even-sized
  chunks
1 all-purpose potato, chopped
1 onion, chopped
1 carrot, chopped

2 teaspoons ground cumin
1 teaspoon freshly grated nutmeg
750 ml (26 fl oz/3 cups) chicken or
  vegetable stock
60 ml (2 fl oz/¼ cup) pouring cream
1 tablespoon chopped flat-leaf
  (Italian) parsley, to garnish

• Put the pumpkin, potato, onion and carrot in the slow cooker. Sprinkle over
the cumin and nutmeg and season with salt and freshly ground black pepper.
Stir to coat the vegetables in the spices. Pour over the stock. Cook on high for
3 hours, or until the pumpkin is tender.

• Using a hand-held stick blender, purée until smooth.
Alternatively, transfer to a food processor and purée
until smooth. Drizzle with cream and scatter
over the parsley before serving.

PEA AND HAM SOUP

preparation time 15 minutes
cooking time 8 hours
serves 6–8

2 onions, finely chopped
2 carrots, finely chopped
2 celery stalks, finely chopped
1 turnip, finely chopped
440 g (15½ oz/2 cups) split green
   peas, rinsed and drained

1 smoked ham hock (800 g/
   1 lb 12 oz) (see Note)
1 litre (35 fl oz/4 cups) chicken stock
2 bay leaves
2 thyme sprigs

• Put the onion, carrot, celery, turnip, peas, ham hock, stock, bay leaves, thyme and 1 litre water (35 fl oz/4 cups) in the slow cooker. Cook on low for 8 hours, or until the peas are very soft and the ham is falling off the bone.

• Remove ham bones and meat. When cool enough to handle, cut off any meat still attached to bone, then cut it into small pieces. Return the meat to the soup. Season to taste with salt and freshly ground black pepper.

Note   *Ask your butcher to cut the ham hock into smaller pieces for you.*

TOMATO, SPINACH AND RISONI SOUP

preparation time 15 minutes
cooking time 3^1/$_2$ hours
serves 4

1 leek, white part only, thinly sliced
1 garlic clove, crushed
^{1}/$_2$ teaspoon ground cumin
500 g (1 lb 2 oz/2 cups) tomato
    passata (puréed tomatoes)
750 ml (26 fl oz/3 cups) chicken or
    vegetable stock
200 g (7 oz/1 cup) risoni (see Note)
200 g (7 oz) smoked ham, chopped
    (optional)
500 g (1 lb 2 oz) English spinach,
    trimmed, leaves sliced
1^1/$_2$ tablespoons lemon juice

Soups

• Put the leek, garlic, cumin, passata, stock and 500 ml (17 fl oz/2 cups) water
in the slow cooker. Cook on low for 3 hours.

• Place the risoni in a heatproof bowl and cover with boiling water. Set aside
for 10 minutes, then drain. Add to the slow cooker along with the ham (if using).
Cook for a further 30 minutes, or until the risoni is tender.

• Stir through the spinach and lemon juice and cook, stirring, until the spinach
is wilted. Season to taste with salt and freshly ground black pepper and serve
with crusty bread.

*Note   Risoni looks like rice but is actually a type of pasta, often used in soups and stews.
If unavailable, use any type of small soup pasta.*

MINESTRONE

preparation time 30 minutes
cooking time 8¹/₂ hours
serves 6–8

1 onion, finely chopped
2 garlic cloves, crushed
80 g (2³/₄ oz) pancetta or bacon,
   diced
1 carrot, diced
2 all-purpose potatoes, cut into 1 cm
   (¹/₂ inch) dice
1 celery stalk, halved lengthways,
   sliced
700 g (1 lb 9 oz) tomato passata
   (puréed tomatoes)
750 ml (26 fl oz/3 cups) chicken or
   vegetable stock

100 g (3¹/₂ oz) ditalini or macaroni
   pasta
100 g (3¹/₂ oz) green beans, cut
   into 2 cm (³/₄ inch) pieces
100 g (3¹/₂ oz) English spinach
   leaves, shredded
400 g (14 oz) tinned cannellini
   beans, drained and rinsed
1 small handful basil, torn
1 small handful flat-leaf (Italian)
   parsley, roughly chopped
freshly grated parmesan cheese,
   to serve

- Put onion, garlic, pancetta, carrot, potato, celery, tomato passata, stock and 750 ml (26 fl oz/3 cups) water in the slow cooker. Cook on low for 8 hours.

- Put the pasta in a heatproof bowl, cover with boiling water and then soak for 10 minutes. Drain.

- Add the drained pasta, green beans, spinach and cannellini beans to the slow cooker. Cook, uncovered, for a further 30 minutes, or until the pasta is al dente and the vegetables are tender.

- Stir through the basil and parsley and season to taste with salt and freshly ground black pepper. Ladle soup into bowls and sprinkle with the parmesan. Serve with crusty bread.

RAVIOLI SOUP

preparation time 20 minutes
cooking time 3–4 hours
serves 4

1 small leek, white part only
3 silverbeet (Swiss chard) leaves
1 carrot, diced
1 zucchini (courgette), diced
1 celery stalk, including some leaves,
    diced

2 whole dried Chinese mushrooms
1.5 litres (52 fl oz/6 cups) chicken
    stock
1 tablespoon light soy sauce
250 g (9 oz) fresh ravioli pasta, such
    as chicken and mushroom

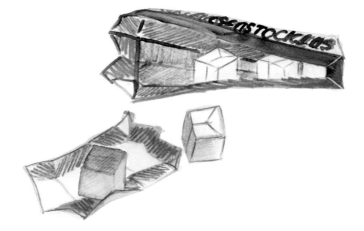

● Leave the root attached to the leek and slice lengthways a few times. Wash thoroughly under cold water to remove any grit, then drain. Chop into small pieces, discarding the root.

● Wash silverbeet leaves and cut away the thick white stems. Tear the leaves into smaller pieces. Set aside.

● Put the leek, carrot, zucchini and celery in the slow cooker. Add the Chinese mushrooms and pour in the stock and soy sauce. Cook on high for 3–4 hours, or until vegetables are cooked. About 30 minutes before the end of cooking time, add the silverbeet and ravioli. Cover and continue to cook for 20 minutes until the pasta is al dente.

● Using kitchen tongs, remove the mushrooms, discard the stems, then thinly slice the mushroom caps and return them to the soup. To serve, ladle the soup and pasta into serving bowls and sprinkle with freshly ground black pepper.

note   *For a vegetarian version, use vegetable stock and a vegetable-filled ravioli.*

BOUILLABAISSE

preparation time 30 minutes
cooking time 6 hours
serves 6

2 tomatoes
1 carrot, chopped
1 celery stalk, chopped
1 leek, white part only, chopped
1 fennel bulb, roughly chopped
250 ml (9 fl oz/1 cup) fish stock
100 ml (3¹/₂ fl oz) white wine or
    Pernod
2 garlic cloves, crushed
grated zest of 1 orange

pinch saffron threads
1 tablespoon tomato paste
    (concentrated purée)
200 g (7 oz) firm white fish fillets,
    such as monkfish
200 g (7 oz) salmon fillet
12 mussels
12 raw prawns (shrimp)
chopped flat-leaf (Italian) parsley,
    to serve

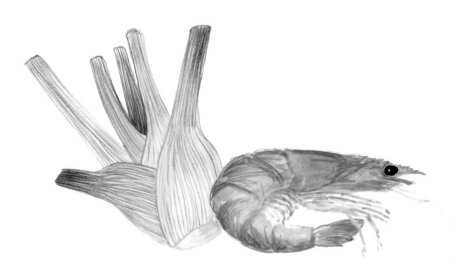

- Score a cross in the base of each tomato. Put the tomatoes in a heatproof bowl and cover with boiling water. Leave for 30 seconds, then transfer to cold water, drain and peel the skin away from the cross. Cut the tomatoes in half and roughly chop the flesh.

- Put tomatoes in slow cooker along with the carrot, celery, leek, fennel, stock, wine, garlic, orange zest, saffron and tomato paste. Cook on high for 3 hours.

- Meanwhile, prepare the seafood. Cut white fish into 2 cm (3/4 inch) pieces. Remove any bones from the salmon using your fingers or a pair of tweezers, and cut into 2 cm (3/4 inch) pieces. Scrub the mussels with a stiff brush and pull out the hairy beards. Discard any broken mussels or open ones that don't close when tapped on the work surface. Peel prawns, leaving the tails intact, then gently pull out the dark vein from each prawn back, starting at the head end. Refrigerate the seafood until needed.

- After 3 hours cooking time, allow the soup base to cool slightly, then transfer the mixture to a food processor and blend until smooth. Return to slow cooker along with the white fish and salmon and cook for a further 2 hours on low.

- Add the mussels and prawns to the slow cooker and then cook for a further 1 hour on low heat. Ladle the soup into large serving bowls and garnish with parsley. Serve with crusty bread.

SEAFOOD CHOWDER

preparation time 30 minutes
cooking time 3¹/₂ hours
serves 4–6

500 g (1 lb 2 oz) skinless firm white
   fish fillets (see Note)
100 g (3¹/₂ oz) smoked ham, diced
3 large all-purpose potatoes, cut into
   1 cm (¹/₂ inch) dice
2 leeks, white part only, thinly sliced
3 large garlic cloves, crushed
1.125 litres (39 fl oz/4¹/₂ cups) fish or
   chicken stock

1 bay leaf
3 thyme sprigs
20 scallops (about 350 g/12 oz),
   without roe 290 g (10¹/₄ oz)
   tinned baby clams, undrained
430 ml (15 fl oz/1³/₄ cups) thick
   (double/heavy) cream
2 tablespoons chopped flat-leaf
   (Italian) parsley

● Cut the fish fillets into 2 cm (³/₄ inch) cubes, then cover and refrigerate until needed.

● Put ham, potato, leek, garlic, stock, bay leaf and thyme in the slow cooker. Cook on high for 3 hours, or until the potato is tender.

● Add fish, scallops, clams and the liquor, and the cream. Cook for a further 30 minutes, or until the fish is cooked. Season to taste with salt and freshly ground black pepper. Stir in the parsley and serve with bread.

Note   *You can use any white fish fillets, such as swordfish or gemfish.*

THAI CHICKEN AND GALANGAL SOUP

preparation time 20 minutes
cooking time 2 hours
serves 4

2 x 5 cm ($3/4$ x 2 inch) piece galangal,
    thinly sliced
500 ml (17 fl oz/2 cups) coconut milk
250 ml (9 fl oz/1 cup) chicken stock
4 makrut (kaffir lime) leaves, torn
1 tablespoon finely chopped
    coriander (cilantro) root, well
    rinsed
1–2 teaspoons finely chopped
    red chilli

500 g (1 lb 2 oz) boneless, skinless
    chicken breasts
2 tablespoons fish sauce
1$1/2$ tablespoons lime juice
3 teaspoons grated palm sugar
    (jaggery) or soft brown sugar
coriander (cilantro) leaves, to garnish

• Put the galangal, coconut milk, stock, half the lime leaves, coriander root and chilli in the slow cooker. Simmer on low for 1$3/4$ hours.

• Meanwhile, prepare the chicken. Trim off any fat and then cut the chicken into thin strips. Add chicken strips, fish sauce, lime juice and palm sugar to the slow cooker and cook for a further 5–10 minutes, or until chicken is cooked through. Stir through remaining lime leaves.

• Ladle the soup into serving bowls and garnish with the coriander leaves.

Soups

TOM YUM

preparation time 30 minutes
cooking time 2 hours
serves 4

3 lemon grass stems, white part only
5–7 bird's eye chillies
3 thin slices galangal
2 litres (70 fl oz/8 cups) chicken stock
   or water
5 makrut (kaffir lime) leaves, torn
350 g (12 oz) raw prawns (shrimp)

90 g (3¹/₄ oz/¹/₂ cup) drained tinned
   straw mushrooms, or quartered
   button mushrooms
2 tablespoons fish sauce
60 ml (2 fl oz/¹/₄ cup) lime juice
2 teaspoons caster (superfine) sugar
coriander (cilantro) leaves, to garnish

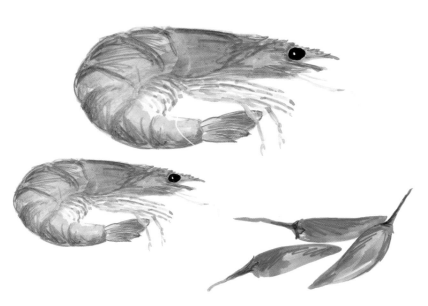

● Use the handle of a knife or a rolling pin to bruise white part of the lemon grass stems. Remove the stems from the chillies and bruise them with the knife handle or rolling pin.

● Place the lemon grass, chillies, galangal, stock and 3 of the lime leaves in the slow cooker. Cook on high for 2 hours.

● Meanwhile, prepare the prawns. Peel prawns, leaving the tails intact. Gently pull out the dark vein from each prawn back, starting at the head end. Add the prawns and mushrooms to the slow cooker and cook for 5 minutes, or until the prawns are firm and pink. Stir through fish sauce, lime juice and sugar. Taste, then adjust seasoning with extra lime juice or fish sauce if necessary. Garnish the soup with coriander leaves before serving.

CHICKEN LAKSA

preparation time 30 minutes
cooking time 2¹/₂ hours
serves 4

CHICKEN BALLS

500 g (1 lb 2 oz) minced (ground)
  chicken
1 small red chilli, finely chopped
2 garlic cloves, finely chopped
¹/₂ small red onion, finely chopped
1 lemon grass stem, white part only,
  finely chopped
2 tablespoons chopped coriander
  (cilantro) leaves
70 g (2¹/₂ oz/¹/₄ cup) laksa paste

750 ml (26 fl oz/3 cups) chicken
  stock
500 ml (17 fl oz/2 cups) coconut
  milk
200 g (7 oz) dried rice vermicelli
  noodles
8 fried tofu puffs, halved
  diagonally
90 g (3¹/₄ oz/1 cup) bean sprouts
2 tablespoons shredded
  Vietnamese mint
3 tablespoons coriander (cilantro)
  leaves
lime wedges, to serve

● To make the chicken balls, put the chicken, chilli, garlic, onion, lemon grass and chopped coriander in a food processor and process until just combined. Roll tablespoons of the mixture into balls with wet hands.

● Put the chicken balls, laksa paste, stock and coconut milk in the slow cooker. Cook on high for 2¹/₂ hours.

● Put the vermicelli in a heatproof bowl, cover with boiling water and soak for 10 minutes. Drain well.

● Divide the vermicelli, tofu puffs and bean sprouts among four serving bowls and ladle the soup over the top, dividing the chicken balls evenly. Garnish with the mint and coriander and serve with the lime wedges.

CURRIED CHICKEN NOODLE SOUP

preparation time 25 minutes
cooking time 2 hours
serves 6

1 small red chilli, seeded and finely
   chopped
1 tablespoon finely chopped fresh
   ginger
2 tablespoons Indian curry powder
750 ml (26 fl oz/3 cups) good-quality
   chicken stock
800 ml (28 fl oz) tinned coconut milk

120 g (4¼ oz) dried rice vermicelli
   noodles
300 g (10½ oz) baby bok choy
   (pak choy)
2 x 250 g (9 oz) boneless, skinless
   chicken breasts
4 tablespoons torn basil

● Put the chilli, ginger, curry powder, stock and coconut milk in the slow cooker.
Cook on high for 1½ hours.

● Meanwhile, prepare the remaining ingredients. Put vermicelli in a heatproof
bowl, cover with boiling water and soak for 10 minutes, or until soft, then drain.
Separate bok choy leaves and slice the large leaves in half lengthways. Prepare
the chicken by trimming off any fat, then cut it into thin slices.

● Stir the vermicelli, bok choy and chicken through the soup. Cook for a further
20 minutes, or until the chicken is tender and cooked. Stir through the basil
just before serving.

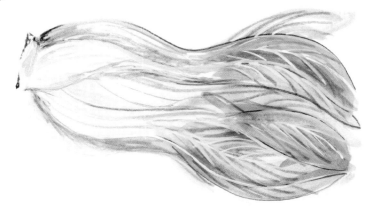

MULLIGATAWNY SOUP

preparation time 30 minutes
cooking time 3–4 hours
serves 4

375 g (13 oz) boneless, skinless
    chicken thighs
2 tablespoons tomato chutney
1 tablespoon mild Indian curry paste
2 teaspoons lemon juice
$^1/_2$ teaspoon ground turmeric
1.25 litres (44 fl oz/5 cups) chicken
    stock
1 onion, finely chopped
1 all-purpose potato, diced
1 carrot, diced
1 celery stalk, diced
65 g (2$^1/_4$ oz/$^1/_3$ cup) basmati rice
2 tablespoons chopped coriander
    (cilantro) leaves

Soups

- Prepare the chicken by trimming off any fat, then cutting into small cubes.

- Put the tomato chutney, curry paste, lemon juice and turmeric in the slow cooker and mix with some of the stock. Add remaining stock. Add the chicken, onion, potato, carrot, celery and rice. Cook on high for 3–4 hours, or until the chicken, vegetables and rice are cooked.

- Season to taste with salt and freshly ground black pepper. Ladle the soup into bowls and serve garnished with the coriander.

Note Add a little more Indian curry paste if you prefer a stronger curry flavour.

CREAMY CHICKEN AND CORN SOUP

preparation time 20 minutes
cooking time 2$1/4$ hours
serves 4–6

4 corn cobs
500 g (1 lb 2 oz) boneless, skinless
   chicken thighs, trimmed
2 garlic cloves, chopped
1 leek, white part only, chopped
1 large celery stalk, chopped
1 bay leaf

$1/2$ teaspoon thyme
1 litre (35 fl oz/4 cups) chicken stock
60 ml (2 fl oz/$1/4$ cup) sherry
1 large floury potato, such as russet, cut
   into 1 cm ($1/2$ inch) dice
185 ml (6 fl oz/$3/4$ cup) pouring cream
snipped chives, to garnish

● Using a large knife, remove the corn kernels from the cobs. Put the corn, chicken, garlic, leek, celery, bay leaf, thyme, stock, sherry and potato in the slow cooker. Cook on high for 2 hours.

● Using kitchen tongs, remove chicken to a board and allow to cool. Discard the bay leaf.

● Purée the soup using a hand-held stick blender. When the chicken is cool enough to handle, shred it and return meat to the slow cooker, then pour in cream. Cook for a further 10–15 minutes, or until chicken is heated through. Garnish with chives before serving.

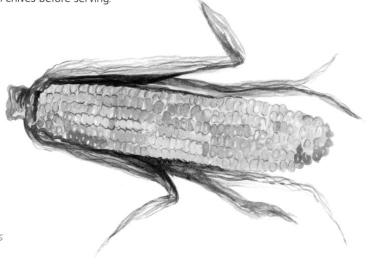

CHICKEN SOUP

preparation time 20 minutes
cooking time 8 hours
serves 6

1.6 kg (3 lb 8 oz) chicken
1 leek, white part only, sliced
2 celery stalks, sliced
1 large carrot, chopped
1 parsnip, chopped
1 tablespoon chopped dill

● Put the chicken, leek, celery, carrot and parsnip in the slow cooker. Cover the chicken and vegetables with 2.5 litres (87 fl oz/10 cups) water or stock. Cook on low for 8 hours, or until the chicken meat is falling off the bones.

● Remove chicken and, when cool enough to handle, remove meat from the bones. Return chicken meat to slow cooker and cook for 5 minutes, or until heated through. Sprinkle with dill to serve.

note   If desired, transfer to a container and refrigerate overnight, then skim the fat from the top the next day.

Soups

BEEF PHO

preparation time 20 minutes
cooking time 6 hours
serves 6

500 g (1 lb 2 oz) piece gravy beef
5 cm (2 inch) piece fresh ginger, thinly
    sliced
1.5 litres (52 fl oz/6 cups) beef stock
6 black peppercorns
1 cinnamon stick
4 cloves
6 coriander seeds
500 g (1 lb 2 oz) fresh thick rice
    noodles
2 tablespoons fish sauce
150 g (5¹/₂ oz) rump steak, very thinly
    sliced
3 spring onions (scallions), finely
    chopped

1 onion, very thinly sliced
3 tablespoons coriander (cilantro)
    leaves
chilli sauce or hoisin sauce, to serve

GARNISHES
red chillies, sliced
bean sprouts
purple basil leaves
spring onions (scallions), sliced
    diagonally
thin lime wedges

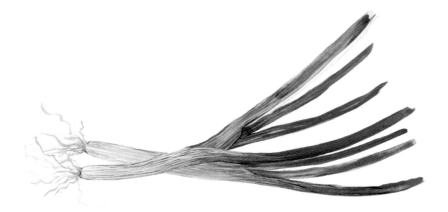

• Put the piece of gravy beef, ginger, stock, peppercorns, cinnamon stick, cloves, coriander seeds, 250 ml (9 fl oz/1 cup) water, and 1 teaspoon salt in the slow cooker. Cook on low for 6 hours.

• Using kitchen tongs, remove beef and set aside to cool. Use a slotted spoon to remove the spices. When the beef is cool enough to touch, cut it across the grain into very thin slices. Set aside.

• Add the rice noodles and fish sauce to the stock in the slow cooker. Cover and cook for 5 minutes, or until the noodles have softened.

• Divide the noodles among the serving bowls. Place some slices of cooked beef and a few slices of raw steak on top of noodles. Ladle hot stock over the top and sprinkle with spring onion, onion slices and coriander leaves.

• Arrange the garnishes on a platter in the centre of the table for each person to choose from. Serve with chilli or hoisin sauce to add to the soup, if desired.

BORSCHT BEEF

preparation time 20 minutes
cooking time 4^1/$_2$–5 hours
serves 4–6

1.2 kg (2 lb 10 oz) chuck steak
1 onion, cut into 2 cm (^{3}/$_4$ inch) dice
2 celery stalks, cut into 2 cm (^{3}/$_4$ inch)
   dice
2 beetroot (beets), peeled and cut
   into wedges
^{1}/$_2$ small cabbage, cut into 2 cm
   (^{3}/$_4$ inch) dice
3 tablespoons tomato paste
   (concentrated purée)

400 g (14 oz) tinned chopped
   tomatoes
375 ml (13 fl oz/1^1/$_2$ cups) beef stock
2 tablespoons vinegar
125 g (4^1/$_2$ oz/^{1}/$_2$ cup) sour cream
2 tablespoons horseradish
squeeze of lemon juice
2 tablespoons chopped flat-leaf
   (Italian) parsley

● Trim the beef of any fat and cut it into 2 cm (³/4 inch) cubes. Combine beef, onion, celery, beetroot, cabbage, tomato paste, tomatoes, stock and vinegar in the slow cooker. Cook on high for 3 hours.

● Remove lid and continue to cook on high for a further 1¹/2–2 hours, or until the borscht reaches a thick casserole consistency. Season to taste with salt and freshly ground black pepper.

● Combine sour cream, horseradish and lemon juice in a bowl and season with salt. Serve soup garnished with the horseradish cream and chopped parsley.

Home cooking

From vegetarians to meat lovers, the slow cooker comes up trumps in providing a sustaining meal.

SPIRALI WITH HAM, LEMON AND PEAS

preparation time 20 minutes
cooking time 3^1/$_4$ hours
serves 6

500 g (1 lb 2 oz) spirali pasta
750 ml (26 fl oz/3 cups) chicken stock
250 ml (9 fl oz/1 cup) pouring cream
3 small thyme sprigs
1 large strip lemon zest
150 g (5^1/$_2$ oz) smoked ham, diced

2 eggs, lightly beaten
100 g (3^1/$_2$ oz/1 cup) freshly grated
   parmesan cheese
230 g (8 oz/1^1/$_2$ cups) fresh or frozen
   peas

● Put the spirali in a large heatproof bowl. Pour over boiling water and set aside, stirring occasionally, for 10 minutes.

● Drain pasta and place it in the slow cooker along with the stock, 625 ml (21 fl oz/2^1/$_2$ cups) water, cream, thyme and strip of lemon zest. Cook on low for 3 hours, or until the liquid has almost absorbed and the pasta is tender.

● Stir in the ham, eggs, parmesan and peas. Cook, stirring occasionally, for 5–10 minutes, or until the peas are cooked and the sauce has thickened. Season to taste with salt and freshly ground black pepper before serving.

ZUCCHINI AND RICOTTA CANNELLONI

preparation time 20 minutes
cooking time 3 hours
serves 4-6

2 zucchini (courgettes), grated
500 g (1 lb 2 oz) fresh ricotta cheese
2 teaspoons chopped rosemary
200 g (7 oz) dried cannelloni (about
    20 tubes)
700 g (1 lb 9 oz) ready-made tomato
    pasta sauce
225 g (8 oz/1^{1}/$_{2}$ cups) grated
    mozzarella cheese
1 handful basil, chopped

- Combine the zucchini, ricotta and rosemary in a bowl. Season with salt and freshly ground black pepper. Use a teaspoon to fill the cannelloni tubes with the zucchini and ricotta mixture.

- Place half of the filled cannelloni in the base of the slow cooker. Pour over half of the tomato pasta sauce to cover and then sprinkle with half the cheese and half the basil. Top with another layer of filled cannelloni and the remaining pasta sauce, cheese and basil.

- Cook on high for 3 hours, or until the pasta is *al dente* and the cheese has melted. Serve with a green salad if desired.

Home cooking

MACARONI CHEESE

preparation time 25 minutes
cooking time 2–3 hours
serves 4–6

200 g (7 oz/2 cups) macaroni pasta
cooking oil spray
375 ml (13 oz) tinned evaporated
 milk
375 ml (13 fl oz/1^1/2 cups) full cream
 milk
3 eggs, lightly beaten
^{1}/2 teaspoon freshly grated nutmeg
3 spring onions (scallions), chopped

125 g (4^1/2 oz) tinned corn kernels,
 drained
60 g (2^1/4 oz) thinly sliced ham,
 chopped
185 g (6^1/2 oz/1^1/2 cups) grated
 cheddar cheese
100 g (3^1/2 oz/1 cup) grated
 parmesan cheese
snipped chives, to garnish

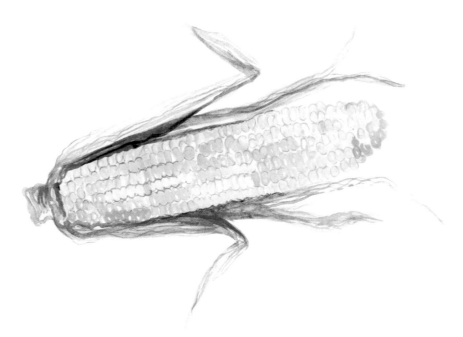

- Put the pasta in a large heatproof bowl. Pour over boiling water and then set aside, stirring occasionally, for 10 minutes. Drain.

- Spray or grease the slow cooker bowl with cooking oil or butter.

- Combine evaporated milk, egg and nutmeg in the slow cooker. Season with salt and freshly ground black pepper. Stir in drained pasta, spring onion, corn, ham, 125 g (4^1/$_2$ oz/1 cup) of the cheddar cheese and all of the parmesan cheese. Sprinkle over the remaining cheddar.

- Cook on low for 2–3 hours. Take care not to overcook it — the sauce will still be a little wet in the centre. If cooked for too long, the sauce will curdle, so start checking after 2 hours — the pasta should be *al dente* and sauce should be thick. Spoon out onto serving plates, sprinkle with chives and serve with a salad.

Note   Cook this recipe on low heat only. Leave out the ham for a vegetarian meal.

GREEK-STYLE STUFFED EGGPLANT

preparation time 20 minutes
cooking time 6 hours
serves 4

2 large eggplants (aubergines)
1 onion, finely chopped
2 garlic cloves, chopped
350 g (12 oz) minced (ground) lamb
60 g (2¼ oz/¼ cup) tomato paste
   (concentrated purée)
185 ml (6 fl oz/¾ cup) red wine

400 g (14 oz) tinned chopped
   tomatoes
250 ml (9 fl oz/1 cup) chicken stock
2 bay leaves
1 cinnamon stick
1 tablespoon dried oregano
Greek-style yoghurt, to serve

- Halve eggplants lengthways. Use a sharp knife to cut a deep circle around the flesh, about 1 cm (¹/₂ inch) in from the edge. Use a large spoon to scoop out the eggplant flesh, then roughly chop the flesh.

- Place eggplant flesh in a bowl along with onion, garlic, lamb and tomato paste. Season with salt and freshly ground black pepper. Mix well to combine.

- Stuff mixture into the hole in the eggplants, reserving any left-over stuffing, and place the filled eggplants in the slow cooker. Pour over the wine, tomatoes and stock and add the bay leaves, cinnamon stick, oregano and any remaining eggplant stuffing. Cook on low for 6 hours, or until the eggplants are tender.

- Remove eggplants to a serving platter. Season to taste with salt and freshly ground black pepper. Serve topped with a dollop of yoghurt and a Greek salad.

CREAMY TOMATO AND CHICKEN STEW

preparation time 20 minutes
cooking time 4 hours
serves 4

1.5 kg (3 lb 5 oz) chicken pieces, trimmed of excess fat
4 bacon slices, fat removed, roughly chopped
2 onions, chopped
1 garlic clove, crushed
400 g (14 oz) tinned chopped tomatoes

300 g (10^{1}/$_{2}$ oz) small button mushrooms, halved
250 ml (9 fl oz/1 cup) pouring cream
2 tablespoons chopped flat-leaf (Italian) parsley
2 tablespoons lemon thyme

● Put the chicken, bacon, onion, garlic and tomatoes in the slow cooker. Cook on high for 3 hours, or until the chicken is nearly tender.

● Add mushrooms and cream and cook for a further 30 minutes, then remove lid and cook for another 30 minutes to thicken sauce. Stir through the parsley and lemon thyme. Serve with mashed potatoes and green beans.

CHICKEN GOULASH

preparation time 20 minutes
cooking time 4³/₄ hours
serves 4

700 g (1 lb 9 oz) boneless, skinless
   chicken thighs
1 onion, sliced
2 garlic cloves, sliced
2 green capsicums (peppers), seeded
   and sliced
1 tablespoon sweet paprika
125 g (4¹/₂ oz/¹/₂ cup) tomato passata
   (puréed tomatoes)

1 marjoram sprig
125 ml (4 fl oz/¹/₂ cup) white wine
250 ml (9 fl oz/1 cup) chicken stock
125 g (4¹/₂ oz/¹/₂ cup) sour cream or
   crème fraîche
1 tablespoon cornflour (cornstarch)
1 small handful flat-leaf (Italian)
   parsley

- Trim the chicken of any fat and cut each thigh into quarters. Put the chicken pieces, onion, garlic, capsicum, paprika, tomato passata and marjoram in the slow cooker. Pour in the wine and stock. Cook on low for 4¹/₂ hours, or until the chicken is tender.

- Combine the sour cream and cornflour in a small bowl. Stir into the chicken mixture in the slow cooker. Cook for a further 5–10 minutes, or until thickened. Season to taste with salt and freshly ground black pepper, and stir through the parsley. Serve the goulash with rice.

Home cooking

APRICOT CHICKEN

preparation time 15 minutes +
cooking time 4 hours
serves 4

4 x 280 g (10 oz) boneless, skinless
    chicken breasts
1 garlic clove, crushed
1 tablespoon grated fresh ginger
1 tablespoon ground cumin
1 tablespoon ground coriander
1 teaspoon ground cinnamon
2 tablespoons vegetable oil
30 g (1 oz/¼ cup) plain (all-purpose)
    flour

400 ml (14 fl oz) tinned apricot
    nectar
1 tablespoon honey
1 tablespoon lemon juice
60 g (2¼ oz/½ cup) slivered
    almonds, toasted
1 handful coriander (cilantro) leaves

● Put the chicken, garlic, ginger, cumin, coriander, cinnamon and oil in a flat
dish. Toss to thoroughly coat the chicken in the oil and spices. Cover and then
refrigerate overnight.

● Put flour in a flat dish. Remove chicken from the marinade and dust with the
flour. Place the chicken in the slow cooker with the apricot nectar, honey and
lemon juice. Cook on high for 4 hours, or until the chicken is cooked through.

● Season to taste with salt and freshly ground black pepper. Top with toasted
almonds and coriander and serve with rice.

CHICKEN CASSEROLE WITH MUSTARD AND TARRAGON

preparation time 20 minutes
cooking time 3 hours
serves 4-6

1 kg (2 lb 4 oz) boneless, skinless
   chicken thighs
1 onion, finely chopped
1 leek, white part only, thinly sliced
1 garlic clove, finely chopped
$^1/_2$ teaspoon dried tarragon
125 ml (4 fl oz/$^1/_2$ cup) chicken stock
350 g (12 oz) button mushrooms,
   sliced
185 ml (6 fl oz/$^3/_4$ cup) pouring cream
2 tablespoons dijon mustard
$1^1/_2$ tablespoons lemon juice

Home cooking

• Trim chicken of any fat, then cut into quarters. Put the chicken pieces, onion, leek, garlic, tarragon and stock in the slow cooker. Cook on high for 2$^1/_2$ hours.

• Add the mushrooms, cream and mustard. Stir to combine, then cook for a further 30 minutes. Stir through the lemon juice. Serve with mashed potatoes and zucchini or green beans.

BASQUE CHICKEN

preparation time 25 minutes
cooking time 8 hours.
serves 4

1.8 kg (4 lb) chicken or chicken pieces
1 onion, cut into 2 cm (3/4 inch) dice
1 red capsicum (pepper), cut into
   2 cm (3/4 inch) dice
1 green capsicum (pepper), cut into
   2 cm (3/4 inch) dice
2 garlic cloves, finely chopped
200 g (7 oz) chorizo sausage, sliced

150 ml (5 fl oz) white wine
80 g (2 3/4 oz) tomato paste
   (concentrated purée)
90 g (3 1/4 oz/1/2 cup) black olives
1/4 preserved lemon
2 tablespoons chopped basil
2 tablespoons chopped parsley

● Joint chicken into eight pieces by removing both legs and cutting between the joint of the drumstick and the thigh. Cut down either side of backbone and lift it out. Turn chicken over and cut through the cartilage down the centre of the breastbone. Cut each breast in half, leaving the wing attached to top half.

● Combine the chicken pieces, onion, red and green capsicum, garlic, chorizo, wine, tomato paste and olives in the slow cooker.

● Rinse the preserved lemon well, remove and discard pulp and membrane and finely dice the rind. Add to chicken and cook on low for 8 hours, or until cooked through.

● Stir through basil and sprinkle with the parsley. Serve with rice if desired.

TURKEY POT ROAST

preparation time 20 minutes
cooking time 4$^3/_4$ hours
serves 6

1.5 kg (3 lb 5 oz) frozen turkey breast
   roll
1 onion, cut into wedges
300 g (10$^1/_2$ oz) orange sweet potato,
   cut into 3 cm (1$^1/_4$ inch) pieces
125 ml (4 fl oz/$^1/_2$ cup) white wine

125 ml (4 fl oz/$^1/_2$ cup) chicken stock
2 zucchini (courgettes), cut into 2 cm
   ($^3/_4$ inch) slices
160 g (5$^1/_2$ oz/$^1/_2$ cup) redcurrant jelly
1 tablespoon cornflour (cornstarch)

- Thaw turkey according to the packet instructions. Remove the elastic string from the turkey and tie up securely with kitchen string, at regular intervals, to retain its shape.

- Put turkey in the slow cooker. Put the onion and sweet potato around the turkey, then pour over the wine and stock. Cook on low for 4 hours.

- Add zucchini and redcurrant jelly. Remove the lid, increase heat to high and cook for a further 30 minutes. Transfer turkey and vegetables to a plate, cover and keep warm.

- Combine the cornflour and 1 tablespoon water in a small bowl and stir until smooth. Add cornflour mixture to the slow cooker and cook, stirring, on high heat for about 10 minutes, or until sauce thickens. Slice the turkey and serve with the vegetables and sauce.

SPANISH-STYLE PORK AND VEGETABLE STEW

preparation time 25 minutes
cooking time 4 hours
serves 4–6

1 kg (2 lb 4 oz) boneless pork
   shoulder
2 hot chorizo sausages, sliced
600 g (1 lb 5 oz) potatoes, cubed
1 red onion, diced
2 garlic cloves, chopped
2 red capsicums (peppers), seeded
   and chopped
400 g (14 oz) tinned chopped
   tomatoes
pinch saffron threads

1 tablespoon sweet paprika
10 large thyme sprigs
1 bay leaf
60 g (2¼ oz/¼ cup) tomato paste
   (concentrated purée)
125 ml (4 fl oz/½ cup) white wine
125 ml (4 fl oz/½ cup) chicken stock
2 tablespoons sherry
1 handful parsley, chopped

- Trim pork and cut into 4 cm (1½ inch) cubes. Put the pork, chorizo, potato, onion, garlic, capsicum, tomatoes, saffron, paprika, thyme and bay leaf in the slow cooker.

- Combine tomato paste, wine, stock and sherry in a small bowl and pour over the pork and vegetables. Cook on high for 4 hours, or until the pork is tender.

- Season to taste with salt and freshly ground black pepper. Stir through the parsley and serve.

PORK SAUSAGES CASSOULET

preparation time 15 minutes
cooking time 3$^1/_4$ hours
serves 4

8 thin pork sausages
1 onion, cut into thin wedges
180 g (6$^1/_4$ oz) mushrooms, sliced
2 garlic cloves, chopped
1 teaspoon paprika
400 g (14 oz) tinned chopped
    tomatoes

1 tablespoon tomato paste
    (concentrated purée)
1 tablespoon seeded mustard
400 g (14 oz) tinned butter or red
    kidney beans, drained and rinsed
2 tablespoons chopped parsley

● Prick the sausages all over and put into the slow cooker. Add the onion, mushrooms and garlic and sprinkle over the paprika, salt and freshly ground black pepper. Pour over the tomatoes, tomato paste and mustard.

● Cook on high for 3 hours, or until the sausages are cooked through. Stir in the beans and cook for a further 15 minutes, or until the beans are heated through. Scatter with parsley before serving.

ɳote   You can brown off the sausages in a non-stick frying pan before adding them to the slow cooker if preferred.

Home cooking

SPARE RIBS WITH BEER AND BARBECUE SAUCE

preparation time 20 minutes
cooking time 4–5 hours
serves 4–6

1.5 kg (3 lb 5 oz) pork spare ribs
185 ml (6 fl oz/¾ cup) beer
185 ml (6 fl oz/¾ cup) barbecue
   sauce
2 tablespoons sweet chilli sauce
1 tablespoon worcestershire sauce
1 tablespoon honey

2 spring onions (scallions), thinly
   sliced
2 garlic cloves, crushed
1 tablespoon cornflour (cornstarch)
1 small handful coriander (cilantro)
   leaves, to garnish

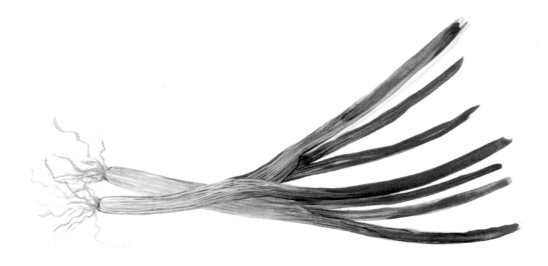

• Cut the ribs into individual ribs, or into sets of two or three if preferred, and trim away any excess fat.

• In a large bowl, combine beer, barbecue sauce, sweet chilli sauce, honey, worcestershire sauce, spring onion and garlic. Season with salt and freshly ground black pepper. Add the ribs and thoroughly coat them in the sauce.

• Transfer the ribs and marinade to slow cooker. Cook on high for 4−5 hours. After 4 hours, check to see if the ribs are tender but the meat should not be falling off the bone. If necessary, continue to cook for the extra hour.

• Using kitchen tongs, remove ribs to a side plate and cover to keep warm. Mix the cornflour with 1 tablespoon water and stir into the sauce in the slow cooker. Cook on high heat for 5−10 minutes, stirring, or until the sauce has thickened.

• Serve the ribs piled onto plates and spoon over some of the sauce. Sprinkle over the coriander leaves. Supply lots of paper napkins for sticky fingers.

SWEET PAPRIKA VEAL GOULASH

preparation time 20 minutes
cooking time 4 hours
serves 4

1 kg (2 lb 4 oz) boneless veal
    shoulder
1 onion, sliced
2 garlic cloves, crushed
1 tablespoon sweet paprika
1/2 teaspoon caraway seeds
2 bay leaves
625 g (1 lb 6 oz/2 1/2 cups) tomato
    passata (puréed tomatoes)

125 ml (4 fl oz/ 1/2 cup) chicken stock
125 ml (4 fl oz/ 1/2 cup) red wine
2 all-purpose potatoes, diced
275 g (9 3/4 oz) jar roasted red
    capsicums (peppers), drained
    and rinsed
sour cream, to serve

● Cut veal into 3 cm (1 1/4 inch) cubes. Put veal, onion, garlic, paprika, caraway seeds, bay leaves, tomato passata, stock, red wine and potatoes in slow cooker. Cook on high for 4 hours, or until the veal is tender. Stir through the capsicum and cook for a further 5 minutes, or until warmed through.

● Taste and season with salt and freshly ground black pepper. Serve with a dollop of sour cream and with cooked fettuccine noodles.

VEAL WITH SWEET POTATO, TOMATO AND OLIVES

preparation time 15 minutes
cooking time 4¹/4 hours
serves 4

1 kg (2 lb 4 oz) piece veal (rump)
350 g (12 oz) orange sweet potato
1 large red onion, chopped
1 celery stalk, chopped
2 garlic cloves, chopped
400 g (14 oz) tinned chopped
    tomatoes
60 ml (2 fl oz/¹/4 cup) white wine

2 tablespoons tomato paste
    (concentrated purée)
1 rosemary sprig
1 tablespoon cornflour (cornstarch)
12 pitted or stuffed green olives
2 tablespoons chopped parsley
grated zest of 1 small lemon

● Cut the veal into 4 cm (1¹/2 inch) cubes. Peel the sweet potato and then cut it into 4 cm (1¹/2 inch) cubes.

● Put the veal, sweet potato, onion, celery, garlic, tomatoes, wine, tomato paste and rosemary in slow cooker. Season with salt and freshly ground black pepper. Cook on high for 4 hours, or until veal is tender and cooked through. Remove the rosemary sprig.

● Combine the cornflour with a little water to make a smooth paste and stir it into the veal. Cook for a further 5–10 minutes to thicken the juices a little. Stir through olives and sprinkle with the chopped parsley and lemon zest to serve.

Home cooking

MEATLOAF WITH TOMATO SAUCE GLAZE

preparation time 30 minutes
cooking time 5–6 hours
serves 4–6

TOMATO SAUCE GLAZE

250 g (9 oz/1 cup) tomato sauce
(ketchup)
2 tablespoons tomato chutney
1 tablespoon soft brown sugar
2 teaspoons worcestershire sauce
1 teaspoon mustard powder

MEATLOAF

1 carrot, diced
1 celery stalk, diced
1 red or green capsicum (pepper),
seeded and diced
4 spring onions (scallions), chopped
155 g (5^{1}/2 oz/1 cup) fresh or frozen
peas
1 kg (2 lb 4 oz) minced (ground) beef
1 teaspoon dried oregano
2 slices wholegrain bread, crusts
removed, diced
2 eggs, lightly beaten
cooking oil spray

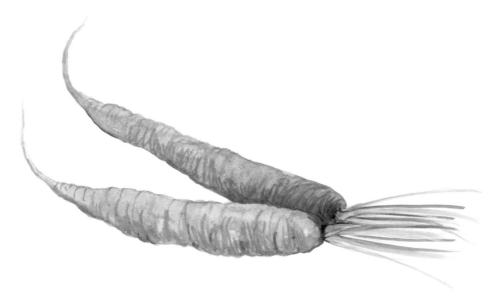

- To make tomato sauce glaze, combine the tomato sauce, chutney, brown sugar, worcestershire sauce and mustard in a small bowl. Set aside.

- To make the meatloaf, combine the carrot, celery, capsicum, spring onion and peas in a large bowl, then add the beef, oregano and diced bread. Season well with salt and freshly ground black pepper. Using clean hands, thoroughly combine the mixture.

- Add about a quarter of the tomato sauce glaze to the beef mixture along with beaten egg and thoroughly mix again. Set aside the rest of the tomato sauce glaze.

- Spray the slow cooker bowl with cooking oil spray or lightly grease with butter or oil. Cut a sheet of foil long enough to fit across the base and up both sides of the bowl, fold it into four lengthways and place across the centre of the bowl.

- Press beef mixture evenly into the slow cooker bowl and smooth the surface. Fold down the foil ends if necessary so the lid can be placed on securely. Cover with the lid and cook on low for 5–6 hours, or until meatloaf is cooked through and has left the side of the bowl.

- To serve, use the foil 'handles' to carefully lift meatloaf onto a serving plate. Heat the reserved tomato sauce glaze in slow cooker and pour over meatloaf. Cut into thick slices and serve with mashed sweet potato and a green salad.

Home cooking

ITALIAN BEEF CASSEROLE WITH DUMPLINGS

preparation time 30 minutes
cooking time 4¹/2 hours
serves 4–6

1 kg (2 lb 4 oz) chuck, blade or
    skirt steak
1 onion, sliced
2 garlic cloves, crushed
250 ml (9 fl oz/1 cup) beef stock
2 x 425 g (15 oz) tins chopped
    tomatoes
450 g (1 lb) jar roasted red capsicums
    (peppers), drained and thickly
    sliced
1 tablespoon chopped oregano
90 g (3¹/4 oz/¹/3 cup) ready-made
    pesto, to serve

DUMPLINGS
40 g (1¹/2 oz/¹/3 cup) plain
    (all-purpose) flour
35 g (1¹/4 oz/¹/4 cup) polenta
1 teaspoon baking powder
1 egg white
2 tablespoons milk
1 tablespoon olive oil

• Trim beef and cut into 3 cm (1 1/4 inch) cubes. Put beef cubes, onion, garlic, stock, tomatoes, capsicum and oregano in slow cooker. Season with salt and freshly ground black pepper. Cook on high for 4 hours, or until beef is tender.

• To make the dumplings, combine the flour, polenta, 1/2 teaspoon salt and baking powder in a large bowl. Make a well in centre and add egg white, milk and olive oil. Stir well to combine. Using teaspoonfuls of the polenta mixture, form it into small balls. Add dumplings to slow cooker and cook for a further 30 minutes, or until the dumplings are cooked through.

• Check the seasoning and add extra salt and pepper if needed. Serve the casserole and dumplings topped with a dollop of pesto.

CURRIED SAUSAGES WITH POTATOES AND PEAS

preparation time 20 minutes
cooking time 4 hours
serves 4

1 tablespoon red lentils
1 teaspoon black peppercorns
1 small dried red chilli, roughly
   chopped
$1/2$ teaspoon cumin seeds
$1/2$ teaspoon coriander seeds
3 all-purpose potatoes, cut into 3 cm
   ($1^1/4$ inch) pieces
1 onion, thickly sliced
500 g (1 lb 2 oz) beef or pork
   sausages

2 fresh curry leaves (optional)
2 tablespoons brandy
60 ml (2 fl oz/$^1/4$ cup) beef stock
1 tablespoon dijon mustard
100 ml ($3^1/2$ fl oz) pouring cream
155 g ($5^1/2$ oz/1 cup) fresh or frozen
   peas
1 handful flat-leaf (Italian) parsley,
   chopped
tomato relish, to serve

- Using a mortar and pestle or spice grinder, pound or grind the lentils, chilli, peppercorns, cumin seeds and coriander seeds to a fine powder. Push powder through a fine strainer and set aside.

- Put the potato and onion in the base of the slow cooker and top with the sausages and curry leaves, if using. Combine brandy, beef stock, mustard and cream and pour over sausages. Cook on low for 4 hours, or until the sausages are cooked through. Stir in the peas and cook for a further 5 minutes, or until the peas are tender.

- Season to taste with salt and freshly ground black pepper. Stir through the parsley and serve with tomato relish.

COUNTRY BEEF STEW

preparation time 30 minutes
cooking time 5¹/₂ hours
serves 6–8

1 kg (2 lb 4 oz) chuck, blade or skirt
   steak
1 small eggplant (aubergine), cut into
   1.5 cm (⁵/₈ inch) cubes
250 g (9 oz) baby new potatoes,
   halved
2 celery stalks, sliced
3 carrots, chopped
2 red onions, sliced
6 ripe tomatoes, chopped
2 garlic cloves, crushed

1 teaspoon ground coriander
¹/₂ teaspoon allspice
³/₄ teaspoon sweet paprika
250 ml (9 fl oz/1 cup) red wine
500 ml (17 fl oz/2 cups) beef stock
2 tablespoons tomato paste
   (concentrated purée)
2 bay leaves
3 tablespoons flat-leaf (Italian)
   parsley, chopped

● Trim the beef and cut it into 4 cm (1¹/₂ inch) cubes. Put the beef in the slow cooker along with the eggplant, potato, celery, carrot, onion, tomato, coriander, garlic, allspice, paprika, wine, stock, tomato paste and bay leaves. Cook on low for 5¹/₂ hours, or until the beef is tender and cooked through.

● Season to taste with salt and freshly ground black pepper. Stir through the parsley and serve.

MINTED BEEF AND TURNIP STEW

preparation time 15 minutes
cooking time 4 hours
serves 4–6

1 kg (2 lb 4 oz) chuck steak
2 onions, thinly sliced
4 small turnips, cut into wedges
150 g (5^1/$_2$ oz) bacon slices, diced
125 ml (4 fl oz/^{1}/$_2$ cup) red wine
1^1/$_2$ tablespoons red wine vinegar
250 ml (9 fl oz/1 cup) beef stock
1 large mint sprig

● Trim beef and cut it into 4 cm (1^1/$_2$ inch) cubes. Put the beef, onion, turnip, bacon, wine, vinegar, stock and mint in slow cooker. Cook on low for 4 hours, or until the beef is tender.

● Remove mint sprig. Season to taste with salt and freshly ground black pepper and serve with crusty bread.

Home cooking

ITALIAN MEATBALLS WITH TOMATO SAUCE

preparation time 25 minutes
cooking time 4 hours
serves 4–6

MEATBALLS

1 onion, finely chopped
80 g (2³⁄4 oz/¹⁄2 cup) pine nuts, roughly chopped
2 garlic cloves, crushed
1 small handful flat-leaf (Italian) parsley, roughly chopped
1 teaspoon chopped rosemary
2 teaspoons fennel seeds, ground
55 g (2 oz/²⁄3 cup) fresh breadcrumbs

25 g (1 oz/¹⁄4 cup) freshly grated parmesan cheese
grated zest of 1 large lemon
1 egg
500 g (1 lb 2 oz) minced (ground) pork or beef
700 g (1 lb 9 oz) tomato passata (puréed tomatoes)
125 ml (4 fl oz/¹⁄2 cup) red wine

- To make meatballs, combine all the ingredients in a bowl. Use your hands to mix well. Roll the mixture into walnut-sized balls and place on a tray. Refrigerate the meatballs for 20 minutes.

- Put tomato passata, wine and meatballs in slow cooker. Season with salt and freshly ground black pepper and cook on high for 4 hours, or until meatballs are cooked through and tender.

- Serve meatballs and tomato sauce with spaghetti, rice or mashed potatoes, and a side salad.

BRAISED BEEF SHORT RIBS

preparation time 15 minutes
cooking time 4–5 hours
serves 6

2 kg (4 lb 8 oz) beef short ribs
180 g (6½ oz) bacon slices
2 onions, chopped
1 garlic clove, crushed
1 small red chilli, seeded and thinly
    sliced
500 ml (17 fl oz/2 cups) beef stock
400 g (14 oz) tinned chopped
    tomatoes
8 bulb spring onions (scallions),
    trimmed and leaves removed

2 strips lemon zest, white pith
    removed
1 teaspoon mild paprika
1 teaspoon chopped rosemary
1 bay leaf
1 tablespoon soft brown sugar
1 teaspoon worcestershire sauce
2 tablespoons chopped basil
2 tablespoons chopped flat-leaf
    (Italian) parsley

● Chop ribs into 4 cm (1½ inch) lengths. Remove rind and fat from the bacon
and cut into 5 mm (¼ inch) dice.

● Put the ribs, bacon, onion, garlic, chilli, stock, tomatoes, spring onions, strips
of lemon zest, paprika, rosemary, bay leaf, brown sugar and the worcestershire
sauce in slow cooker. Cook on high for 4–5 hours, or until the ribs are tender.

● Skim off as much fat as you can from top. Stir through the basil and parsley.
Serve the ribs with mashed potatoes or soft polenta if desired.

BEEF CARBONNADE

preparation time 15 minutes
cooking time 4 hours
serves 4

1.2 kg (2 lb 10 oz) chuck steak
3 onions, chopped
1 garlic clove, crushed
1 teaspoon soft brown sugar
375 ml (13 fl oz/1½ cups) beer (bitter
    or stout)

2 bay leaves
4 thyme sprigs
2 tablespoons plain (all-purpose) flour
1 handful flat-leaf (Italian) parsley,
    chopped

● Trim the beef of excess fat and cut into 4 cm (1½ inch) cubes. Put the beef, onion, garlic, brown sugar, beer, bay leaves, thyme and flour in the slow cooker and stir to combine. Season with freshly ground black pepper. Cook on high for 4 hours, or until the beef is cooked through.

● Season to taste with salt and extra pepper if desired, and sprinkle with the parsley. Serve with green beans or zucchini.

Home cooking

71

CORNED BEEF WITH CABBAGE AND POTATOES

preparation time 20 minutes
cooking time 8–10 hours
serves 4–6

1.5 kg (3 lb 5 oz) piece corned beef
   (silverside)
1 small onion
8 whole cloves
500 g (1 lb 2 oz) small new potatoes
   (about 12)
1 tablespoon soft brown sugar
1 tablespoon malt vinegar
8 black peppercorns
2 bay leaves
500 g (1 lb 2 oz) savoy cabbage, core
   attached and cut into 4–6 wedges

MUSTARD AND PARSLEY SAUCE

1 egg
2 tablespoons caster (superfine) sugar
1 tablespoon plain (all-purpose) flour
1 teaspoon mustard powder
60 ml (2 fl oz/¼ cup) malt vinegar
2 tablespoons finely chopped flat-leaf
   (Italian) parsley

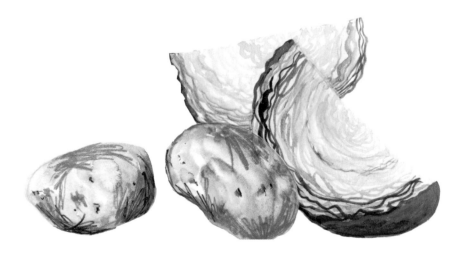

- Rinse corned beef, pat dry with paper towel and then trim off any excess fat. Peel the onion and stud it with the cloves.

- Put the potatoes in slow cooker in a single layer and top with corned beef. Barely cover with cold water. Add onion, the combined brown sugar and malt vinegar, peppercorns and bay leaves.

- Cook on low for 8–10 hours, or until beef is tender. About 45 minutes before the end of cooking time, arrange the cabbage wedges around the meat, cover and cook until cabbage is tender. When beef is cooked, remove to a side plate and cover with foil to keep warm.

- To make mustard and parsley sauce, remove 250 ml (9 fl oz/1 cup) of the cooking liquid from the slow cooker and set aside. Whisk together the egg and sugar in a small bowl, then whisk in the flour and mustard powder. Gradually add the reserved cooking liquid and vinegar, mixing until smooth. Pour into a small saucepan and stir over medium heat until thickened. Stir through parsley.

- To serve, cut the corned beef into thick slices. Use a slotted spoon to lift the potatoes and cabbage out of the slow cooker to the serving plates. Discard the onion. Serve with the mustard and parsley sauce and with some steamed carrots and green beans if desired.

Note *Store left-over corned beef in a bowl with the remaining cooking liquid to cover. Cover with plastic wrap and refrigerate.*

GREEK LAMB WITH MACARONI

preparation time 30 minutes
cooking time 2^1/$_4$ hours
serves 4–6

1 kg (2 lb 4 oz) boneless lamb leg
1 large onion, chopped
2 garlic cloves, crushed
400 g (14 oz) tinned chopped
   tomatoes
60 g (2^1/$_4$ oz/^{1}/$_4$ cup) tomato paste
   (concentrated purée)

500 ml (17 fl oz/2 cups) beef stock
2 tablespoons red wine vinegar
1 tablespoon soft brown sugar
1 teaspoon dried oregano
200 g (7 oz/2 cups) macaroni pasta
125 g (4^1/$_2$ oz) pecorino cheese,
   grated

• Trim the lamb of any excess fat and cut into 3 cm (1^1/$_4$ inch) cubes. Put the lamb, onion, garlic, tomatoes, tomato paste, stock, vinegar, brown sugar and the oregano in the slow cooker. Cook on high for 1^3/$_4$ hours, or until lamb is tender.

• Place the macaroni in a large heatproof bowl and cover with boiling water. Set aside for 10 minutes. Drain and add macaroni to slow cooker and stir to combine. Cook for a further 30 minutes, or until the pasta is tender and the liquid has absorbed.

• Divide among serving bowls and sprinkle with the cheese.

BRAISED LAMB WITH CAPSICUM AND FENNEL

preparation time 15 minutes
cooking time $4^{1}/4$ hours
serves 4

1 kg (2 lb 4 oz) lamb shoulder or leg
1 large onion, chopped
1 red capsicum (pepper), seeded and
    sliced into strips
1 yellow capsicum (pepper), seeded
    and sliced into strips
2 fennel bulbs, trimmed and each cut
    into thick slices lengthways
4 garlic cloves, chopped

250 ml (9 fl oz/1 cup) tomato passata
    (puréed tomatoes)
60 ml (2 fl oz/$^{1}/4$ cup) beef stock or
    water
1 tablespoon tomato paste
    (concentrated purée)
1 teaspoon worcestershire sauce
1 tablespoon cornflour (cornstarch)
fennel fronds, to garnish

● Trim the lamb of any excess fat and cut into 4 cm (1 $^{1}/2$ inch) cubes. Put
lamb, onion, red and yellow capsicum, fennel, garlic, tomato passata, stock,
tomato paste and worcestershire sauce in slow cooker. Season with salt and
freshly ground black pepper. Cook on high for 4 hours, or until the lamb is
tender and cooked through.

● Combine the cornflour with a little water to make a smooth paste and stir it
into the lamb. Cook for a further 5–10 minutes to thicken the juices a little.

● To serve, divide the lamb among the serving bowls and scatter over some
chopped fennel fronds.

Home cooking

75

LANCASHIRE HOTPOT

preparation time 15 minutes
cooking time 4 hours
serves 4

4 all-purpose potatoes, sliced
6 baby onions, peeled and left whole
1 tablespoon thyme, chopped
1 kg (2 lb 4 oz) lamb shoulder chops
2 tablespoons worcestershire sauce
125 ml (4 fl oz/1/2 cup) beef stock
1 handful flat-leaf (Italian) parsley,
    chopped

● In a large bowl, toss together the potato, onions and thyme. Layer the potato and onions in the base of the slow cooker and top with the lamb chops. Pour over the worcestershire sauce and stock. Cook on high for 4 hours, or until the lamb is tender and cooked through.

● Season with salt and freshly ground black pepper, and stir through parsley before serving.

GREEK LEG OF LAMB WITH OREGANO

preparation time 15 minutes
cooking time 10 hours
serves 6

1.8 kg (4 lb) lamb leg
1 tablespoon dried oregano
8 small all-purpose potatoes, such as
    coliban, peeled and halved
400 g (14 oz) tinned chopped
    tomatoes
80 ml (2¹/₂ fl oz/¹/₃ cup) red wine

250 ml (9 fl oz/1 cup) chicken stock
1 strip lemon zest, white pith
    removed
2 bay leaves
1 tablespoon lemon juice
2 tablespoons chopped fresh oregano

● Put the lamb leg in the slow cooker and sprinkle with dried oregano. Scatter potatoes around lamb. Add tomatoes, wine, stock and 250 ml (9 fl oz/1 cup) water. Season with freshly ground black pepper and add the strip of lemon zest and the bay leaves. Cook on low for 10 hours, or until lamb is cooked through.

● Remove the lamb and potatoes and transfer to a platter. Skim fat from the surface of sauce and stir through lemon juice and fresh oregano. Season the sauce with salt and freshly ground black pepper, then pour over lamb to serve.

Home cooking

77

CHUTNEY CHOPS WITH POTATOES AND PEAS

preparation time 15 minutes
cooking time 4 hours
serves 4

1.2 kg (2 lb 10 oz) lamb forequarter
   chops
4 all-purpose potatoes, such as
   desiree, sliced
2 garlic cloves, crushed
240 g (8^1/$_2$ oz) jar tomato fruit
   chutney

400 g (14 oz) tinned chopped
   tomatoes
125 ml (4 fl oz/^{1}/$_2$ cup) red wine
125 ml (4 fl oz/^{1}/$_2$ cup) chicken stock
2 rosemary sprigs
80 g (2^3/$_4$ oz/^{1}/$_2$ cup) fresh or frozen
   peas

● Trim lamb chops of excess fat. Layer chops and potato slices in slow cooker.

● Combine the garlic, chutney, tomatoes, wine, stock and rosemary and add to the slow cooker. Cook on high for 4 hours, or until the potato is tender and the meat is falling from the bones.

● Stir through the peas and cook for a further 5 minutes. Season to taste with salt and freshly ground black pepper before serving.

IRISH STEW

preparation time 25 minutes
cooking time 4^1/$_2$ hours
serves 6

600 g (1 lb 5 oz) all-purpose
   potatoes, thickly sliced
3 carrots, thickly sliced
1 onion, cut into 16 wedges
1 small leek, white part only, thickly
   sliced
150 g (5^1/$_2$ oz) savoy cabbage, thinly
   sliced

4 bacon slices, cut into strips
8 lamb neck chops
375 ml (13 fl oz/1^1/$_2$ cups) beef stock
2 tablespoons finely chopped flat-leaf
   (Italian) parsley

• Layer half the potato, carrot, onion, leek, cabbage and bacon in the base of the slow cooker. Arrange the lamb chops in a single layer over the bacon and cover with layers of the remaining vegetables and bacon. Pour over the stock and cook on low for 4^1/$_2$ hours, or until the lamb is very tender and the sauce is slightly reduced.

• Taste and check for seasoning. Divide among shallow bowls and sprinkle with the parsley. Serve with bread to mop up the juices.

Home cooking

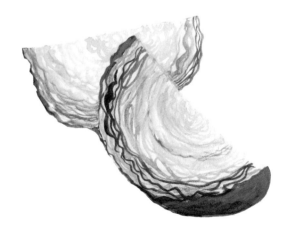

Entertaining

A boon for the busy cook, these recipes
take the hard work out of preparing
something impressive for guests.

SEAFOOD FIDEOS

preparation time 30 minutes
cooking time 3 hours
serves 4–6

300 g (10¹/₂ oz) raw prawns (shrimp)
    300 g (10¹/₂ oz) firm white fish
    fillets
200 g (7 oz) squid tubes
1 kg (2 lb 4 oz) mussels
1 onion, finely chopped
1 garlic clove, finely chopped
400 g (14 oz) tinned whole tomatoes,
    strained (use juice only)

¹/₂ teaspoon chilli flakes
2 tablespoons chopped oregano
125 g (4¹/₂ oz) fideos or vermicelli
    pasta (see Note)
chopped flat-leaf (Italian) parsley, to
    serve
flour tortillas, to serve

• Prepare the seafood. Peel the prawns, leaving the heads and tails intact. Gently pull out the dark vein from each prawn back, starting at the head end. Cut the fish into 3 cm (1 1/4 inch) pieces. Cut squid tubes into 1 cm (1/2 inch) rings. Scrub mussels with a stiff brush and pull out hairy beards. Discard any broken mussels or open ones that don't close when tapped on work surface.

• Put prepared prawns, fish, squid rings, mussels, onion, garlic, tomato juice, chilli and oregano in the slow cooker. Cook on high for 2 hours.

• Break noodles into 5 cm (2 inch) lengths and then place in a large heatproof bowl and cover with boiling water. Set aside to soften for 10 minutes, then drain.

• Place softened noodles on top of seafood in the slow cooker. Cook for 1 hour on low. Transfer the seafood and noodles to a serving dish and sprinkle with the chopped parsley. Serve with warmed flour tortillas.

Note *Fideos is a traditional Mexican or Spanish dish. The word refers to the noodle that is used, which is a very thin, vermicelli-like pasta. If you can't find fideos noodles, use vermicelli or capellini pasta.*

HOWTOWDIE

preparation time 30 minutes
cooking time 4¹/₄ hours
serves 4–6

STUFFING

85 g (3 oz/²/₃ cup) oatmeal
2 tablespoons shredded suet or
   dripping (see Notes)
1 small onion, finely chopped
1¹/₂ tablespoons chopped flat-leaf
   (Italian) parsley
¹/₂ teaspoon finely grated lemon zest
1¹/₂ tablespoons whisky

1.8 kg (4 lb) chicken
1 leek, white part only, sliced
1 bay leaf
very small pinch ground cloves
pinch freshly grated nutmeg
500 ml (17 fl oz/2 cups) chicken stock
1–2 chicken livers, chopped
60 ml (2 fl oz/¹/₄ cup) thick (double/
   heavy) cream

- To make stuffing, toast oatmeal in a frying pan over medium heat until golden and aromatic. Remove to a bowl. Add suet to the pan and, when it is bubbling, add the onion and cook for 5 minutes, or until soft and lightly golden. Add to the bowl with the oatmeal, along with the parsley, lemon zest and whisky. Stir to combine so that mixture is loosely bound. If too dry, add 1 tablespoon water or chicken stock. Season well with salt and freshly ground black pepper and allow to cool completely before stuffing the chicken.

- Rinse chicken inside and out and allow to dry. Loosely fill chicken with the stuffing, then tie or skewer the legs together to secure the stuffing inside the chicken. Put chicken in the slow cooker along with the leek, bay leaf, cloves, nutmeg and stock. Cook on low for 4 hours, or until chicken is tender and the juices run clear when the thigh is pierced with a skewer.

- Carefully lift chicken out of the slow cooker, transfer it to a plate and cover to keep warm while you finish the sauce.

- Purée the chicken livers in the small bowl of a food processor. Remove all but 250 ml (9 fl oz/1 cup) of liquid from the slow cooker. Add the puréed chicken livers to the liquid left in the slow cooker and stir until they melt into sauce. Add cream and cook for a few minutes, or until sauce is heated through, but don't allow it to boil. (For a smoother sauce, strain cooking liquid before adding livers and cream.)

- Serve chicken whole or carved with the sauce poured over and a little of the stuffing on the side. Serve with green vegetables such as blanched green beans and wilted spinach.

Note   Howtowdie is a traditional Scottish recipe of roast chicken with oat stuffing. Suet is a firm, white fat available from most butchers.

CHICKEN AGRODOLCE

preparation time 30 minutes
cooking time 3$^1/_2$ hours
serves 6

1.2 kg (2 lb 10 oz) chicken pieces, skin removed
1 garlic clove
1 tablespoon dried oregano
2 bay leaves
125 ml (4 fl oz/$^1/_2$ cup) red wine vinegar
125 ml (4 fl oz/$^1/_2$ cup) dry white wine

55 g (2 oz/$^1/_4$ cup firmly packed) soft brown sugar
220 g (7$^3/_4$ oz/1 cup) pitted prunes
2 tablespoons capers, rinsed
175 g (6 oz/1 cup) green olives
1 handful flat-leaf (Italian) parsley, chopped

● Combine the chicken, garlic, oregano, bay leaves, vinegar, wine and brown sugar in the slow cooker. Cook on low for 3 hours.

● Stir in prunes, capers and olives and cook for a further 30 minutes, or until chicken is cooked through. Season with salt and freshly ground black pepper and stir through the parsley. Serve with mashed potato.

CHICKEN WITH CELERIAC AND MARJORAM

preparation time 10 minutes
cooking time 3 hours
serves 6

1 kg (2 lb 4 oz) boneless, skinless
    chicken thighs
1 leek, white part only, sliced
1 garlic clove, crushed
1 large celeriac, trimmed, peeled and
    diced

250 ml (9 fl oz/1 cup) chicken stock
2 small marjoram sprigs
300 ml (10^1/$_2$ fl oz) pouring cream
1 handful flat-leaf (Italian) parsley,
    chopped

- Trim the chicken thighs of any fat and cut them into quarters. Combine the
chicken pieces, leek, garlic, celeriac, stock and marjoram in slow cooker. Cook
on high for 2^1/$_2$ hours. Add the cream and cook for a further 30 minutes.

- Season to taste with salt and freshly ground black pepper. Stir through the
parsley and serve with steamed asparagus if desired.

Entertaining

COQ AU VIN

preparation time 15 minutes
cooking time 3³/₄ hours
serves 8

2 x 1.5 kg (3 lb 5 oz) chickens
   (see note)
2 bay leaves
2 thyme sprigs
250 g (9 oz) bacon, diced
20 baby onions, peeled
375 ml (13 fl oz/1¹/₂ cups) red wine
1 litre (35 fl oz/4 cups) chicken stock

125 ml (4 fl oz/¹/₂ cup) brandy
2 teaspoons tomato paste
   (concentrated purée)
250 g (9 oz) button mushrooms
60 g (2¹/₄ oz) butter, softened
40 g (1¹/₂ oz/¹/₃ cup) plain
   (all-purpose) flour

- Joint each chicken into eight pieces by removing both legs and then cutting between the joint of the drumstick and the thigh. Cut down either side of the backbone and lift it out. Turn the chicken over and cut through the cartilage down the centre of the breastbone. Cut each breast in half, leaving the wing attached to the top half.

- Put the chicken pieces, bay leaves, thyme, bacon, onions, wine, stock, brandy and tomato paste in the slow cooker. Cook on high for 3 hours, or until the chicken is almost cooked through.

- Add mushrooms and cook for a further 30 minutes. Lift out the chicken and vegetables and place them on a plate, cover and set aside.

- Mix together the butter and flour and whisk into the sauce in the slow cooker. Cook on high for about 10 minutes, stirring, until thickened, then return chicken and vegetables to the sauce to heat through. Serve with steamed potatoes.

ℕote   *Alternatively, buy 3 kg (6 lb 12 oz) chicken pieces.*

SALMON WITH HORSERADISH CRUST AND PUY LENTILS

preparation time 25 minutes
cooking time 4¹/₄ hours
serves 4

400 g (14 oz/2 cups) puy lentils or
 tiny blue-green lentils
500 ml (17 fl oz/2 cups) vegetable
 stock grated zest and juice of
 1 lemon
1 small green chilli, finely chopped
80 g (2³/₄ oz/1 cup) fresh sourdough
 breadcrumbs
2 tablespoons grated fresh or
 prepared horseradish

4 tablespoons chopped dill
10 g (¹/₄ oz) butter, melted
4 x 180 g (6¹/₂ oz) salmon fillets
50 g (1³/₄ oz) English spinach, stalks
 removed, chopped
1 handful coriander (cilantro) leaves
125 g (4¹/₂ oz/¹/₂ cup) plain yoghurt,
 to serve
lemon wedges, to serve

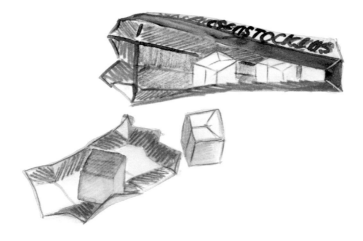

- Put the lentils, stock, lemon zest, lemon juice and chilli in the slow cooker. Cook on high for 3 hours.

- In a food processor, roughly pulse the breadcrumbs and horseradish until well combined. Stir through dill and melted butter until mixture is fairly moist.

- Remove any bones from salmon using your fingers or tweezers, then press the breadcrumb mixture over the top side of the salmon fillets.

- In a large non-stick frying pan over medium heat, cook crumbed side of the salmon for 3 minutes, or until crumbs are golden. Work in batches if necessary.

- Mix spinach through the lentils in the slow cooker and place salmon on top. Cook on low for 1 hour, or until fish is cooked through and flakes when tested with a fork. Remove the salmon to serving plates.

- Mix the coriander through the lentils and spoon some lentils onto each plate. Serve the salmon topped with the yoghurt and with lemon wedges on the side.

CHICKEN WITH TARRAGON AND FENNEL

preparation time 25 minutes
cooking time 6^1/$_4$ hours
serves 6

300 g (10^1/$_2$ oz) kipfler (fingerling)
   potatoes
1 large fennel bulb
1 red onion
1.8 kg (4 lb) chicken
1 lemon
2–3 tablespoons extra virgin olive oil

4 garlic cloves, finely chopped
3 tarragon sprigs
125 ml (4 fl oz/^{1}/$_2$ cup) chicken stock
125 ml (4 fl oz/^{1}/$_2$ cup) verjuice
250 g (9 oz) cherry tomatoes
2 tablespoons chopped flat-leaf
   (Italian) parsley

- Peel the potatoes and then cut them into 2 cm ($3/4$ inch) pieces. Cover with water and set aside.

- Remove the tough outer shell of the fennel. Slice into 8–10 wedges, leaving the root section attached so each fennel wedge doesn't fall apart. Peel onion and cut into 8–10 wedges, again using root section to hold wedges together.

- Rinse chicken inside and out and pat dry with paper towel. Cut the lemon in half and place in the chicken cavity. Sprinkle the chicken with salt and set aside.

- Heat the oil in a heavy-based non-stick frying pan over medium heat. Add the fennel and the onion wedges and then cook, in batches if necessary, for about 5 minutes until golden brown. Add garlic, reduce heat to low and cook for about 2 minutes, or until lightly browned.

- Drain the potatoes and put them in the slow cooker along with the fennel, onion and garlic. Top with the tarragon.

- Return frying pan to medium heat, add the whole chicken and cook, turning until browned all over, for about 3 minutes each side. Place browned chicken on top of the vegetables in the slow cooker. Pour in the stock, verjuice and add the tomatoes. Cook on low for 6 hours, or until the chicken is cooked through and tender and the juices run clear when the thigh is pierced with a skewer.

- Season to taste with salt and freshly ground black pepper and then sprinkle with the chopped parsley.

SPANISH-STYLE DUCK WITH PEARS

preparation time 30 minutes
cooking time 5^1/$_4$ hours
serves 4

2 kg (4 lb 8 oz) duck
^{1}/$_4$ teaspoon freshly grated nutmeg
^{1}/$_2$ teaspoon smoked paprika
pinch ground cloves
2 firm ripe pears, peeled, quartered
   and cored
8 French shallots, peeled
8 baby carrots, trimmed
2 garlic cloves, sliced

1 bay leaf
1 thyme sprig
1 cinnamon stick
80 ml (2^1/$_2$ fl oz/^{1}/$_3$ cup) sherry
750 ml (26 fl oz/3 cups) chicken stock
100 g (3^1/$_2$ oz/^{2}/$_3$ cup) whole
   almonds, toasted
25 g (1 oz) dark bittersweet
   chocolate, roughly chopped

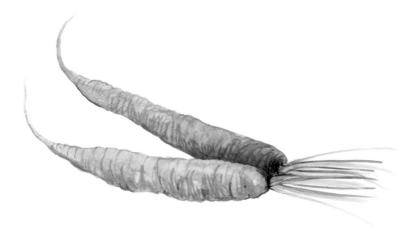

- Trim the duck of excess fat and then joint it into eight pieces.

- In a small bowl, mix together nutmeg, paprika, cloves and a little salt and freshly ground black pepper. Dust the duck pieces with the spice mixture.

- Put the duck in the slow cooker along with pears, shallots and carrots. Add the garlic, bay leaf, thyme, cinnamon stick, sherry and stock. Cook on low for 5 hours, or until the duck is tender and cooked. Skim the surface of any fat.

- Meanwhile, finely grind the almonds and the chocolate in a food processor. Transfer to a bowl.

- When the duck is cooked, lift the duck, pears, shallots, carrots and cinnamon stick out of the liquid using a slotted spoon and transfer to a serving dish. Cover and keep warm.

- Simmer the liquid left in the slow cooker, uncovered, for 10 minutes. Remove 250 ml (9 fl oz/1 cup) of the hot liquid and stir into the ground almonds and chocolate. Whisk chocolate mixture back into liquid in the slow cooker until the sauce has thickened. Season to taste, then pour sauce over the duck and serve.

RABBIT WITH MUSTARD

preparation time 20 minutes
cooking time 3¹/₄ hours
serves 6–8

60 g (2¹/₄ oz/¹/₂ cup) plain
    (all-purpose) flour
2 kg (4 lb 8 oz) farmed rabbit, jointed
1 tablespoon olive oil
20 g (³/₄ oz) butter
200 g (7 oz) bacon, finely chopped
250 ml (9 fl oz/1 cup) white wine
1 onion, finely chopped

2 carrots, finely chopped
1 garlic clove, crushed
250 ml (9 fl oz/1 cup) chicken stock
3 tablespoons dijon mustard
2 bay leaves
300 ml (10¹/₂ fl oz) pouring cream
flat-leaf (Italian) parsley, to garnish

- Put flour in a shallow dish and season well with salt and freshly ground black pepper. Coat rabbit pieces in a dusting of seasoned flour. Heat the oil and butter in a large frying pan over medium heat and cook rabbit pieces for 3–4 minutes each side, or until golden. Transfer to the slow cooker.

- Add the bacon to the frying pan and cook for 5 minutes, or until crisp. Add to the slow cooker. Pour off any fat from pan and deglaze with the wine, stirring well. Pour the wine into the slow cooker.

- Add the onion, carrot, garlic, stock, half of the mustard, the bay leaves and the cream to the slow cooker. Cook on low for 3 hours, or until rabbit is tender and cooked through.

- Stir in rest of mustard and season to taste with salt and freshly ground black pepper. Before serving, sprinkle with parsley. Serve with boiled potatoes.

BRAISED PORK NECK WITH ORANGE AND STAR ANISE

preparation time 30 minutes
cooking time 4$^{1}/_{4}$ hours
serves 6

1 large handful flat-leaf (Italian)
   parsley
1 tablespoon ground cinnamon
1 tablespoon grated fresh ginger
2 garlic cloves, crushed

1.6 kg (3 lb 8 oz) pork neck (pork
   scotch) fillet
1 orange, peeled and segmented
80 ml (2$^{1}/_{2}$ fl oz/$^{1}/_{3}$ cup) olive oil
4 star anise

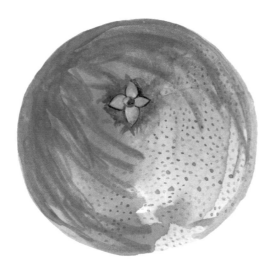

- Put the parsley in a heatproof bowl and pour over enough boiling water to cover. Strain, then transfer the blanched parsley to the small bowl of a food processor along with the cinnamon, ginger and garlic. Process to a paste.

- Slice the pork lengthways along the middle and open it out flat on a clean work surface. Brush with parsley and cinnamon paste and lay orange segments along the centre. Roll the pork tightly to form a cylinder, enclosing the orange, and tie at intervals with kitchen string. Brush pork with olive oil and generously season with sea salt and freshly ground black pepper.

- Heat remaining oil in a large frying pan and seal pork on high for 4 minutes on each side, or until golden all over.

- Put the pork in the slow cooker along with the star anise and cook on high for 4 hours, or until the pork is tender and cooked through. Season with salt and freshly ground black pepper. Serve the pork with mashed sweet potato.

PORK COOKED IN MILK

preparation time 15 minutes
cooking time 6$\frac{1}{4}$ hours
serves 6

2 kg (4 lb 8 oz) pork loin rack, with
   6 chops
6 baby potatoes, peeled and halved
1 large fennel bulb, cut into thick
   wedges

2 garlic cloves, halved lengthways
2 rosemary sprigs
1 litre (35 fl oz/4 cups) milk
grated zest of 2 lemons
juice of 1 lemon

● Trim pork of most of the excess fat. Put the pork, potato, fennel, rosemary, garlic, milk, lemon zest and the lemon juice in the slow cooker. Cook on low for 6 hours, or until the pork is tender.

● Transfer the pork and the vegetables to a serving platter. Cover with foil and set aside to rest for 10 minutes. While pork is resting, increase slow cooker heat to high and reduce the liquid left in the bowl. Taste and check for seasoning.

● Strain the sauce if you like (you don't need to, but it may look curdled) and then serve with the pork and vegetables.

PORK LOIN RACK WITH PANCETTA AND SWEET POTATO

preparation time 20 minutes
cooking time 4–5 hours
serves 4

1.2 kg (2 lb 10 oz) pork loin rack, with 4 chops
90 g (3¼ oz) piece pancetta, 1 cm (½ inch) thick, diced
6 bulb spring onions (scallions), trimmed with 3 cm (1¼ inch) stem, halved lengthways
2 garlic cloves, chopped
350 g (12 oz) purple-skinned sweet potato, chopped into 5 cm (2 inch) chunks

250 ml (9 fl oz/1 cup) sparkling apple juice (cider)
1 cinnamon stick
1 tablespoon cornflour (cornstarch)
2 tablespoons chopped flat-leaf (Italian) parsley

● Trim the pork of skin and fat and press some sea salt and freshly ground black pepper over the pork.

● Put the pork, diced pancetta, spring onions, garlic, sweet potato, apple juice and cinnamon stick in the slow cooker. Cook on high for 4–5 hours, or until the pork is tender. Transfer the pork and vegetables to a serving platter. Cover with foil and allow to rest. Remove the cinnamon stick.

● While pork is resting, combine cornflour with a little water to make a smooth paste and stir into juices in the slow cooker. Cook for a further 5–10 minutes to thicken the juices a little.

● To serve, cut through loin to serve a chop per person. Spoon over vegetables and some juices. Scatter over the parsley.

Entertaining

VEAL OLIVES WITH PROSCIUTTO, CHEESE AND SAGE

preparation time 40 minutes
cooking time 6–8 hours
serves 4

TOMATO AND OLIVE SAUCE

400 g (14 oz) tinned chopped
    tomatoes
2 semi-dried (sun-blushed) tomatoes,
    chopped
2 spring onions (scallions), chopped
2 garlic cloves, crushed
10 black olives, pitted and chopped
1 teaspoon caster (superfine) sugar
6 x 150 g (5½ oz) veal leg steaks
    (schnitzel)

6 prosciutto slices, trimmed of fat
50 g (1¾ oz/½ cup) freshly grated
    parmesan cheese
finely grated zest of 1 lemon
12 sage leaves
1 tablespoon olive oil
20 g (¾ oz) butter
1 tablespoon cornflour (cornstarch)
    (optional)
extra sage leaves, to garnish

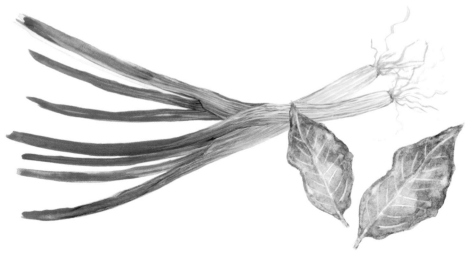

- To make the tomato and olive sauce, combine the tomatoes, semi-dried tomatoes, spring onion, garlic, olives and sugar in a bowl. Season with salt and freshly ground black pepper. Pour half the tomato sauce into the slow cooker and set the remainder aside.

- Put each veal steak between two sheets of plastic wrap and use the flat side of a meat mallet to pound them to around 5 mm ($^1/_4$ inch) thick and roughly 25 x 10 cm (10 x 4 inches) in size.

- Lay the prosciutto slices along the top of each veal steak. Evenly divide the parmesan, lemon zest and sage leaves along each piece of veal. Season with freshly ground black pepper. Roll up veal and secure with a toothpick to form veal olives.

- Heat oil and butter in a large frying pan. When the oil is hot, add veal olives and cook for 5 minutes, turning frequently until browned. Arrange veal olives over the tomato sauce in the slow cooker. They will be packed in side by side. Pour over the remaining tomato sauce. Cook on low for 6–8 hours, or until the veal is tender. Remove veal olives to a side plate and remove toothpicks, cover and keep warm.

- If you like, you can thicken the sauce. Combine 1 tablespoon water with the cornflour in a bowl and mix with until smooth, then stir into the sauce. Stir over high heat until thickened.

- To serve, cut each veal olive into three or four thick slices diagonally and arrange onto serving plates. Pour over sauce and garnish with a sage leaf or two. Serve with mashed potato or polenta and a green vegetable or salad.

Entertaining

VEAL WITH PEPERONATA AND GNOCCHI

preparation time 30 minutes
cooking time 4–6 hours
serves 4

PEPERONATA

400 g (14 oz) tinned whole tomatoes
1 red onion, cut into thin wedges
2 garlic cloves, chopped
1 red or green chilli, seeded and finely
   chopped (optional)
1 red capsicum (pepper), seeded and
   thinly sliced
1 yellow capsicum (pepper), seeded
   and thinly sliced
1 tablespoon red wine vinegar
1 teaspoon caster (superfine) sugar
60 g (2^{1}/$_{4}$ oz/^{1}/$_{2}$ cup) plain
   (all-purpose) flour
4 even-sized pieces (about 750 g/
   1 lb 10 oz) veal osso bucco (see
   Note)
20 g (^{3}/$_{4}$ oz) butter
1 tablespoon olive oil
125 ml (4 fl oz/^{1}/$_{2}$ cup) white wine
350 g (12 oz) packet potato gnocchi

GREMOLATA

grated zest of 1 lemon
1 garlic clove, finely chopped
1 large handful flat-leaf (Italian)
   parsley, finely chopped

- To make the peperonata, put tomatoes in a large bowl and roughly chop with scissors or a knife. Add remaining peperonata ingredients and mix to combine. Season with salt and freshly ground black pepper. Add half of the peperonata to the slow cooker.

- Put the flour in a flat dish and season well with salt and freshly ground black pepper. Trim the osso bucco pieces of excess fat and then coat the veal in the seasoned flour.

- Heat the butter and oil in a large frying pan over medium heat. When the oil is hot, add the osso bucco and brown well for 2–3 minutes on each side. Pour in the wine and let it bubble and reduce a little. Arrange the browned veal in a single layer on top of the peperonata in the slow cooker. Pour in any juices left in the frying pan, then spoon over the remaining peperonata.

- Cook on high for 4–6 hours, or until the veal is very tender. Remove the osso bucco to a side plate, cover and keep warm. Add the gnocchi to the peperonata in slow cooker and stir to combine. Cover and cook for a further 20 minutes, or until the gnocchi is tender.

- To make gremolata, combine lemon zest, garlic and parsley in a small bowl.

- To serve, spoon the gnocchi and peperonata onto serving plates, top with the osso bucco and sprinkle over the gremolata.

Note   Use veal chops instead of veal osso bucco if you prefer.

BRAISED VEAL SHANKS

preparation time 30 minutes
cooking time 4 hours
serves 4–6

4–6 veal shanks (about 2 kg/
    4 lb 8 oz)
200 g (7 oz/1²/₃ cups) plain (all-
    purpose) flour
1 leek, white part only, finely diced
1 onion, finely diced
1 carrot, finely diced
1 celery stalk, finely diced
2 garlic cloves, finely chopped
1 bay leaf
1 rosemary sprig, leaves chopped
125 ml (4 fl oz/¹/₂ cup) red wine
500 ml (17 fl oz/2 cups) veal stock
200 g (7 oz) artichoke halves
80 g (2³/₄ oz/¹/₂ cup) frozen peas

ORANGE GREMOLATA
1 garlic clove, finely chopped
grated zest of 1 orange
1 small handful flat-leaf (Italian)
    parsley, finely chopped

● Coat the veal shanks in the flour and shake off the excess. Put the veal in the slow cooker along with the leek, onion, carrot, celery, garlic, bay leaf, rosemary, wine and stock. Cook on high for 3 hours.

● Add the artichokes to the slow cooker. Continue to cook on high, with the lid off, for 1 hour. Add the peas and cook for a further 5 minutes, or until the peas are cooked through. Season to taste with salt and freshly ground black pepper.

● To make the orange gremolata, combine the garlic, orange zest and parsley. Serve the veal shanks sprinkled with the gremolata.

VEAL, LEMON AND CAPER CASSEROLE

preparation time 25 minutes
cooking time 4 hours
serves 4

300 g (10$^1/_2$ oz) French shallots, unpeeled

1 kg (2 lb 4 oz) boneless veal shoulder

2 garlic cloves, crushed

3 leeks, white part only, cut into large chunks

2 tablespoons plain (all-purpose) flour

500 ml (17 fl oz/2 cups) chicken stock

1 teaspoon grated lemon zest

80 ml (2$^1/_2$ fl oz/$^1/_3$ cup) lemon juice

2 bay leaves

2 tablespoons capers, rinsed well

chopped flat-leaf (Italian) parsley, to serve

caperberries, to garnish (optional)

• Put the shallots in a heatproof bowl. Pour over boiling water to cover and set aside for 5 minutes to soften. Drain and peel.

• Trim veal and cut into 4 cm (1$^1/_2$ inch) cubes. Put the shallots and the veal cubes in the slow cooker along with garlic, leek, flour, stock, lemon zest, lemon juice and bay leaves. Stir to combine ingredients. Cook on high for 4 hours, or until the veal is tender. During the last 30 minutes of cooking, remove the lid to allow the sauce to reduce a little.

• To serve, stir in capers and season with salt and freshly ground black pepper. Sprinkle with parsley and garnish with caperberries if desired.

VEAL WITH LEMON THYME

preparation time 15 minute
cooking time 3$^{1}/_{2}$ hours
serves 4

2 tablespoons olive oil
1.5 kg (3 lb 5 oz) rack of veal
  (6 cutlets), trimmed to a neat
  shape
2 leeks, white part only, thinly sliced
30 g (1 oz) butter

1 tablespoon plain (all-purpose) flour
1 tablespoon grated lemon zest
125 ml (4 fl oz/$^{1}/_{2}$ cup) chicken stock
125 ml (4 fl oz/$^{1}/_{2}$ cup) white wine
2 tablespoons lemon thyme
125 ml (4 fl oz/$^{1}/_{2}$ cup) pouring cream

● Heat oil in a deep heavy-based frying pan over medium heat and brown the
veal well on all sides. Remove the veal from the pan and put in the slow cooker.

● Add the leek and butter to the frying pan, reduce the heat and cook, stirring
occasionally, for 10 minutes, or until soft. Add the flour to the pan and cook for
2 minutes, stirring continuously. Add lemon zest and season with freshly ground
black pepper. Stir in stock and wine and bring to the boil, stirring continuously.
Add leek mixture to the slow cooker. Cook on low for 3 hours, or until the veal
is tender and cooked through.

● Remove veal to a plate, cover and set aside. Increase the slow cooker heat to
high. Add the lemon thyme and cream and then cook, uncovered, for a further
10 minutes. Season with salt and freshly ground black pepper. Serve veal with
the sauce and boiled baby potatoes.

Entertaining

OXTAIL WITH MARMALADE

preparation time 20 minutes +
cooking time 4^1/$_4$ hours
serves 4

1.5 kg (3 lb 5 oz) oxtail
160 g (5^1/$_2$ oz/^{1}/$_2$ cup) marmalade
100 ml (3^1/$_2$ fl oz) sherry
2 tablespoons olive oil
4 all-purpose potatoes, cut into 3 cm
   (1^1/$_4$ inch) pieces

2 carrots, sliced
1 onion, thinly sliced
2 bay leaves
1 cinnamon stick
1 orange, peeled and segmented

● Cut the oxtail into sections, then combine with marmalade and sherry in a large bowl. Cover and marinate overnight.

● Heat the olive oil in a large frying pan over high heat and cook the oxtail in batches for 4 minutes on each side, or until golden brown all over. Set aside.

● Put potato, carrot, onion, bay leaves and cinnamon stick in the slow cooker and sit the oxtail on top. Cook on high for 4 hours, or until the meat is tender. Season with salt and ground black pepper. Top oxtail with the orange segments and serve with mashed potato.

BRAISED BEEF WITH TURNIPS AND HERBS

preparation time 20 minutes
cooking time 4 hours
serves 4–6

1 kg (2 lb 4 oz) chuck steak
150 g (5 1/2 oz) bacon slices, diced
2 onions, thinly sliced
2 large turnips, halved, each half cut
    into 4 wedges
125 ml (4 fl oz/1/2 cup) red wine

250 ml (9 fl oz/1 cup) beef stock
1 1/2 tablespoons red wine vinegar
1 large mint sprig
1 small handful flat-leaf (Italian)
    parsley, chopped

• Trim beef and cut into 4 cm (1 1/2 inch) cubes. Combine beef, bacon, onion, turnips, wine, stock, vinegar and mint in slow cooker. Cook on low for 4 hours.

• Season with salt and freshly ground black pepper. Remove the mint and stir through the parsley. Serve with mashed potato or bread.

PROSCIUTTO-WRAPPED BEEF WITH BROAD BEANS

preparation time 25 minutes +
cooking time 2¹/₂ hours
serves 4

500 g (1 lb 2 oz) thick beef fillet
3 garlic cloves, thinly sliced
2 tablespoons chopped rosemary
8–10 thin slices prosciutto, pancetta
   or smoked bacon
2 tablespoons olive oil
20 g (³/₄ oz) dried wild mushrooms,
   such as porcini

1 onion, halved and sliced
170 ml (5¹/₂ fl oz) red wine
400 g (14 oz) tinned chopped
   tomatoes
400 g (14 oz) peeled broad (fava)
   beans

- Trim the beef of any excess fat and make several small incisions around the beef. Push a slice of garlic into each incision, using up one of the garlic cloves. Sprinkle 1 tablespoon of the rosemary over the beef and season with salt and freshly ground black pepper.

- Lay the prosciutto slices on a board in a line next to each other, creating a sheet of prosciutto to wrap the beef in. Place beef fillet across them and fold the prosciutto over to enclose the beef. Tie several times with kitchen string to keep the beef and prosciutto together. Leave in the refrigerator to rest for at least 15 minutes.

- Heat olive oil in a large frying pan over high heat. Add beef and sear on all sides until prosciutto is golden brown, but not burnt. A little of the prosciutto might fall off, but it doesn't matter just make sure beef is well sealed. Remove from the pan.

- Put dried mushrooms in a bowl with 185 ml (6 fl oz/3/4 cup) hot water and soak for 10 minutes.

- Put the beef in the slow cooker along with the onion, remaining garlic and rosemary, the mushrooms and the soaking liquid, wine and tomatoes. Cook on low for 2 hours, or until the beef is tender.

- Add broad beans and cook for a further 20 minutes. Season with salt and freshly ground black pepper and serve with mashed potato or soft polenta.

BEEF STROGANOFF WITH MIXED MUSHROOMS

preparation time 40 minutes
cooking time 3–4 hours
serves 4

325 g (11$^1/_2$ oz) new potatoes, unpeeled, cut into 1.5 cm ($^5/_8$ inch) thick slices

300 g (10$^1/_2$ oz) mixed mushrooms, such as oyster and Swiss brown, thickly sliced

1 onion, thinly sliced into rings

2–3 garlic cloves, chopped

1 teaspoon dried oregano

750 g (1 lb 10 oz) round or sirloin steak

30 g (1 oz/$^1/_4$ cup) plain (all-purpose) flour

$^1/_2$ teaspoon paprika

2 tablespoons olive oil

125 ml (4 fl oz/$^1/_2$ cup) beef stock

125 ml (4 fl oz/$^1/_2$ cup) white wine

2 tablespoons tomato paste (concentrated purée)

125 g (4$^1/_2$ oz/$^1/_2$ cup) sour cream

1 small handful chopped flat-leaf (Italian) parsley

- Layer the sliced potatoes in the base of the slow cooker.

- Put the mushrooms and the onion in a large bowl. Sprinkle over the garlic and oregano and season well with salt and freshly ground black pepper.

- Trim beef of any fat, then cut it into thin strips across the grain. Pat dry with paper towel. Combine the flour and paprika in a flat dish.

- Heat 2 teaspoons of olive oil in a large frying pan over high heat. Working with a quarter of the meat at a time, dust meat in flour, shake off the excess, then add to pan and toss for 1–2 minutes, or until meat is browned. Transfer to the mushroom and onion mixture. Repeat with remaining oil, beef and flour.

- Add any remaining flour to the frying pan, then pour in the stock, wine and tomato paste and whisk together until hot. Pour over the meat mixture in the bowl and toss well to combine. Transfer to slow cooker over the sliced potatoes. Cook on high for 3–4 hours, or until beef is tender and potatoes are cooked.

- Just before serving, stir through the sour cream and half the parsley. Spoon onto serving plates and serve with potatoes. Sprinkle with remaining parsley.

BEEF OSSO BUCCO

preparation time 30 minutes
cooking time 5–6 hours
serves 4

60 g (2¹/₄ oz/¹/₂ cup) plain
   (all-purpose) flour
1 kg (2 lb 4 oz) beef osso bucco
2–3 tablespoons vegetable oil
1 onion, finely chopped
1 carrot, finely chopped
2 bay leaves
¹/₂ teaspoon black peppercorns
400 g (14 oz) tinned chopped
   tomatoes
185 ml (6 fl oz/³/₄ cup) white wine
155 g (5¹/₂ oz/1 cup) frozen peas
1 handful flat-leaf (Italian) parsley,
   chopped

GREMOLATA
2 garlic cloves, finely chopped
1 handful flat-leaf (Italian) parsley,
   chopped
grated zest of 2 lemons

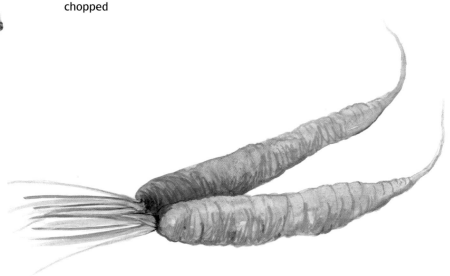

● Put the flour in a flat dish and season with salt and freshly ground black pepper. Dust the osso bucco in the seasoned flour.

● Heat the oil in a large frying pan over medium heat, add the osso bucco in batches and cook for about 5 minutes on each side, or until the osso bucco is golden brown all over.

● Put the onion, carrot, bay leaves, peppercorns and osso bucco in the slow cooker and then pour over tomatoes and wine. Cook on high for 5–6 hours, or until the beef is tender. Add the peas and cook for a further 5 minutes.

● Just before the osso bucco is cooked, make the gremolata. Combine garlic, parsley and lemon zest in a bowl, cover and set aside.

● Before serving, season the beef with salt and freshly ground black pepper and stir through parsley. Transfer to serving plates, sprinkle with gremolata and serve with mashed potatoes and steamed vegetables.

PORTUGUESE BEEF

preparation time 20 minutes
cooking time 5^{1}/$_{4}$ hours
serves 6

1.25 kg (2 lb 12 oz) chuck steak
2 garlic cloves, thinly sliced
175 g (6 oz) smoked bacon slices,
   chopped
250 ml (9 fl oz/1 cup) red wine
250 ml (9 fl oz/1 cup) beef stock
1 tablespoon sweet paprika
^{3}/$_{4}$ teaspoon smoked paprika

2 bay leaves
2 teaspoons dried oregano
20 g (^{3}/$_{4}$ oz) butter, at room
   temperature
2 tablespoons plain (all-purpose) flour
175 g (6 oz/1 cup) green olives
30 g (1 oz/^{1}/$_{4}$ cup) slivered almonds

● Trim beef and cut it into 4 cm (1 ^{1}/$_{2}$ inch) cubes. Put the beef, garlic, bacon, wine, stock, sweet paprika, smoked paprika, bay leaves and oregano in the slow cooker. Cook on low for 5 hours, or until the beef is tender.

● Mix together the butter and the flour. Add gradually to the beef in the slow cooker, stirring. Cook, uncovered, for a further 10 minutes, or until the mixture has thickened.

● Stir through the olives and almonds and season with salt and freshly ground black pepper. Serve with mashed potato or steamed rice.

BEEF WITH ROOT VEGETABLES AND BROAD BEANS

preparation time 20 minutes
cooking time 4 hours
serves 4

1.2 kg (2 lb 10 oz) chuck steak
1/2 teaspoon dried thyme
1 leek, white part only, cut into 1 cm
   (1/2 inch) thick slices
1 celery stalk, sliced
2 garlic cloves, chopped
2 parsnips, quartered
300 g (10 1/2 oz) orange sweet potato,
   cut into 8 wedges

1 swede (rutabaga), cut into 8 wedges
250 ml (9 fl oz/1 cup) red wine
60 ml (2 fl oz/1/4 cup) tomato sauce
   (ketchup)
1 tablespoon cornflour (cornstarch)
175 g (6 oz) frozen broad (fava)
   beans

Entertaining

- Trim beef and cut into 4 cm (1 1/2 inch) cubes. Put beef in the slow cooker, sprinkle over thyme and season well with salt and freshly ground black pepper. Add leek, celery, garlic, parsnip, sweet potato, swede, wine and tomato sauce. Cook on high for 4 hours, or until the beef is tender.

- About 20 minutes before the end of cooking, combine the cornflour with a little water to make a smooth paste and stir it into the beef and the vegetables along with the broad beans. Continue to cook until broad beans are cooked through, then serve.

BEEF CHEEKS WITH ONIONS, MUSHROOMS AND THYME

preparation time 25 minutes
cooking time 8¹/₄ hours
serves 4

1 kg (2 lb 4 oz) beef cheeks
100 g (3¹/₂ oz) bacon or speck, trimmed of fat, chopped
250 ml (9 fl oz/1 cup) red wine
2 celery stalks, finely chopped
1 carrot, finely chopped
1 onion, finely chopped
10 g (¹/₄ oz) thyme

3 garlic cloves
250 ml (9 fl oz/1 cup) beef stock
40 g (1¹/₂ oz) butter
12 baby onions, peeled and trimmed, halved lengthways if large
1¹/₂ tablespoons sugar
1¹/₂ tablespoons sherry vinegar
16 button mushrooms, halved

- Trim beef cheeks of excess fat and sinew, then cut into four portions. Put the beef in the slow cooker along with the bacon, wine, celery, carrot, onion, thyme, garlic and stock. Cook on low heat for 7 hours (this will vary slightly, depending on the thickness of the beef), or until the meat is almost falling apart.

- Meanwhile, place half of the butter in a heavy-based frying pan, add onions and cook over low–medium heat for about 8 minutes, or until golden. Add the sugar and cook until caramelised, shaking the pan occasionally to ensure that it caramelises evenly. Add half the vinegar and stir to remove any sediment from the bottom of the pan. Transfer to the slow cooker.

- Melt the remaining butter in the pan and cook the mushrooms over medium heat for 5–6 minutes, or until golden. Pour in the remaining vinegar and stir to remove any sediment from bottom of pan. Add mushrooms to the slow cooker and cook, uncovered, for a further 1 hour, or until beef is tender and the sauce has reduced and thickened slightly.

- Serve the beef cheeks with the sauce, and with mashed potato and steamed green vegetables.

SLOW-COOKED LAMB IN RED WINE

preparation time 20 minutes +
cooking time 10$^1/_4$ hours
serves 6

2 kg (4 lb 8 oz) lamb leg
50 g (1$^3/_4$ oz) butter, softened
2$^1/_2$ tablespoons plain (all-purpose)
   flour

MARINADE
750 ml (26 fl oz) red wine, such as
   burgundy or cabernet sauvignon
60 ml (2 fl oz/$^1/_4$ cup) brandy
10 garlic cloves, bruised
1 tablespoon chopped rosemary
2 teaspoons chopped thyme
2 fresh bay leaves, torn into small
   pieces
1 large carrot, diced
1 large celery stalk, diced
1 onion, finely chopped
60 ml (2 fl oz/$^1/_4$ cup) olive oil

- Trim any really thick pieces of fat from the lamb but leave it with a decent covering all over if possible.

- Combine marinade ingredients in a non-metallic baking dish, then add the lamb and turn to coat in marinade. Cover and refrigerate for 24–48 hours, turning occasionally so marinade is evenly distributed. Make sure you wrap and rewrap the dish tightly with plastic wrap each time to ensure the strong odours from the marinade do not permeate other foods in the refrigerator.

- Put the lamb and marinade in the slow cooker. Cook on low for 10 hours, or until the lamb is tender and cooked.

- Carefully remove lamb to a serving platter using two wide spatulas. Cover the lamb with foil and a tea towel to keep warm while you make the sauce.

- Drain off the fat from the liquid in the slow cooker. Transfer the ingredients left in the bowl of the slow cooker to a food processor. Purée, then strain liquid back into the slow cooker. Turn the slow cooker heat to high. Mix together the softened butter and flour and gradually whisk it into the sauce. Continue cooking for a further 10–15 minutes, or until sauce has thickened slightly.

- Carve the lamb and serve with the sauce. Serve with green vegetables and potato gratin.

NAVARIN OF LAMB

preparation time 20 minutes
cooking time 3³/4 hours
serves 4

1 kg (2 lb 4 oz) boneless lean lamb
   shoulder
200 g (7 oz) baby turnips
8 bulb spring onions (scallions),
   trimmed
175 g (6 oz) small potatoes, peeled
1 onion, chopped
1 garlic clove, crushed
125 ml (4 fl oz/¹/2 cup) chicken stock
125 ml (4 fl oz/¹/2 cup) red wine

2 tablespoons tomato paste
   (concentrated purée)
1 large rosemary sprig
2 thyme sprigs
1 bay leaf
18 baby carrots
155 g (5¹/2 oz/1 cup) fresh or frozen
   peas
1 tablespoon redcurrant jelly
1 handful parsley, chopped

• Trim the lamb of any excess fat and cut into 3 cm (1¹/4 inch) cubes. Put the lamb, turnips, spring onions, potatoes, onion, garlic, stock, wine, tomato paste, rosemary, thyme and bay leaf in the slow cooker. Stir to combine. Cook on high for 3 hours, or until the lamb is almost tender.

• Trim the carrots, leaving a little bit of green stalk. Add the carrots to the slow cooker and then cook for a further 40 minutes, or until the carrots are tender.

• Stir through the peas, the redcurrant jelly and parsley and cook for a further 5 minutes, or until peas are tender. Season with salt and freshly ground black pepper before serving.

LAMB SHANKS IN RED WINE

preparation time 20 minutes
cooking time 4^1/$_2$ hours
serves 4

1 onion, finely diced
1 leek, white part only, finely diced
1 carrot, finely diced
2 celery stalks, finely diced
1.4 kg (3 lb 2 oz) lamb shanks
  (4 shanks, about 300–350 g/
  10^1/$_2$–12 oz each)
3 garlic cloves, sliced
4 large rosemary sprigs

4 prosciutto slices
60 g (2^1/$_4$ oz/^{1}/$_4$ cup) tomato paste
  (concentrated purée)
500 ml (17 fl oz/2 cups) beef stock
250 ml (9 fl oz/1 cup) red wine
90 g (3^1/$_4$ oz/^{1}/$_2$ cup) black olives
1 small handful parsley, finely
  chopped

- Place the diced vegetables in the base of the slow cooker.

- Make three or four small incisions in meaty part of the lamb shanks. Insert the garlic slices into the incisions. Put a rosemary sprig on each lamb shank and wrap it with a slice of prosciutto. Secure the prosciutto with a toothpick.

- Add lamb shanks to the diced vegetables in the slow cooker. Top with the tomato paste, stock and wine and season with salt and freshly ground black pepper. Cook on high for 4^1/$_2$ hours.

- Add the olives and cook, uncovered, for a further 5 minutes, or until the olives are warmed through. Stir through the parsley and serve.

Entertaining

Hot & spicy

Travel to exotic places without leaving home, with this selection of vibrant, robustly flavoured recipes.

CHICKPEA AND VEGETABLE CURRY

preparation time 30 minutes
cooking time 3–4 hours
serves 4–6

3 garlic cloves, crushed
1 red or green chilli, seeded and
   chopped
2 tablespoons Indian curry paste
1 teaspoon ground cumin
1/2 teaspoon ground turmeric
400 g (14 oz) tinned chopped
   tomatoes
250 ml (9 fl oz/1 cup) vegetable stock
   or water
1 red onion, cut into thin wedges
1 large carrot, sliced diagonally into
   3 cm (1¹/4 inch) chunks
250 g (9 oz) orange sweet potato,
   sliced diagonally into 3 cm
   (1¹/4 inch) chunks

250 g (9 oz) cauliflower, cut into
   florets
250 g (9 oz) broccoli, cut into florets
2 long, thin eggplants (aubergines),
   about 100 g (3¹/2 oz) in total, cut
   into 3 cm (1¹/4 inch) thick slices
400 g (14 oz) tinned chickpeas,
   drained and rinsed
155 g (5¹/2 oz/1 cup) fresh or frozen
   peas
165 ml (5¹/2 fl oz) tinned coconut milk
1 small handful coriander (cilantro)
   leaves, to garnish

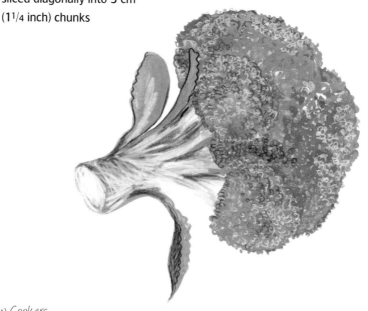

• Combine garlic, chilli, curry paste, cumin, turmeric, tomatoes and stock in the slow cooker. Stir in onion, carrot, sweet potato, cauliflower, broccoli, eggplant and chickpeas. Cook on high for 3–4 hours, or until all the vegetables are cooked.

• Add peas and stir through the coconut milk. Continue to cook for a further 10 minutes, or until the peas are cooked through.

• To serve, ladle the curry into large bowls and then sprinkle with the coriander leaves. Serve with rice.

note *You can add a little more curry paste if you prefer a stronger curry flavour.*

YELLOW CURRY WITH VEGETABLES

preparation time 30 minutes
cooking time 3 hours
serves 4

100 g (3¹/₂ oz) cauliflower
1 long, thin eggplant (aubergine)
1 small red capsicum (pepper)
2 small zucchini (courgettes)
150 g (5¹/₂ oz) green beans
1–2 tablespoons yellow curry paste
500 ml (17 fl oz/2 cups) coconut
   cream
125 ml (4 fl oz/¹/₂ cup) vegetable
   stock

150 g (5¹/₂ oz) baby corn
1¹/₂ tablespoons fish sauce
2 teaspoons grated palm sugar
   (jaggery) or soft brown sugar
1 small red chilli, seeded and
   chopped, to garnish
coriander (cilantro) leaves, to
   garnish

• Prepare vegetables. Cut cauliflower into florets and cut eggplant, capsicum and zucchini into 1 cm (¹/₂ inch) slices. Cut beans into 3 cm (1¹/₄ inch) lengths.

• Put cauliflower, eggplant and capsicum in the slow cooker with curry paste, coconut cream and stock. Cook on low for 2 hours, or until cauliflower is tender.

• Stir in the zucchini, beans, corn, fish sauce and sugar and cook for a further 1 hour, or until the vegetables are tender. Garnish with the chilli and coriander and serve with steamed rice.

DHAL

preparation time 15 minutes
cooking time 4 hours
serves 8

400 g (14 oz/2 cups) red lentils
1 onion, chopped
2 garlic cloves, chopped
2 teaspoons ground turmeric
2 teaspoons finely chopped fresh
    ginger
2 bay leaves
1 cinnamon stick
2 teaspoons ground cumin

1 teaspoon ground coriander
1 teaspoon mustard seeds
750 ml (26 fl oz/3 cups) chicken or
    vegetable stock
1 teaspoon garam masala
40 g (1¹/₂ oz) butter
2 large handfuls coriander (cilantro)
    leaves, chopped

• Put the lentils, onion, garlic, turmeric, ginger, bay leaves, cinnamon stick, cumin, ground coriander, mustard seeds, stock and 1 litre (35 fl oz/4 cups) water in the slow cooker. Cook on low for 4 hours, or until the lentils are soft.

• Stir in the garam masala, butter and coriander leaves. Stir until butter has melted, then serve.

Hot & spicy

SPICY FISH CURRY

preparation time 20 minutes
cooking time 2 1/2 hours
serves 4

400 ml (14 fl oz) tinned coconut milk
5 green chillies, seeded and chopped
2 dried red chillies, chopped into
   pieces
1/2 cinnamon stick
2 teaspoons grated fresh ginger
2 garlic cloves, finely chopped
4 stalks fresh curry leaves (optional)
1 teaspoon ground turmeric
1/4 teaspoon chilli powder

1 teaspoon curry powder
2 tomatoes, finely chopped
250 ml (9 fl oz/1 cup) fish or chicken
   stock
800 g (1 lb 12 oz) snapper fillets,
   cubed
2 spring onions (scallions), sliced
   diagonally
juice of 2 limes, to taste

• Put coconut milk, green and red chilli, cinnamon stick, ginger, garlic, curry leaves (if using), turmeric, chilli powder, curry powder, tomato and stock in the slow cooker. Cook on low for 2 hours, or until the flavours have developed.

• Add the fish and cook for a further 30 minutes, or until the fish is cooked through and flakes when tested with a fork. Stir through half the spring onion and add most of the lime juice, then taste to see if more lime juice is needed. Serve with rice and garnish with the remaining spring onion.

PENANG CHICKEN CURRY

preparation time 10 minutes
cooking time 3 hours
serves 4

RED CURRY PASTE
1 red onion, thickly sliced
10 g (1/4 oz) galangal, sliced
2 garlic cloves, chopped
1 teaspoon chilli powder
2 coriander (cilantro) roots,
    washed well
1 teaspoon shrimp paste

3 tablespoons peanuts, toasted
800 g (1 lb 12 oz) boneless,
    skinless chicken breasts
400 ml (14 fl oz) tinned coconut
    cream
coriander (cilantro) leaves,
    to garnish
sliced red chilli, to garnish

- To make red curry paste, place all the paste ingredients in a food processor and blend until smooth. Alternatively, pound the ingredients using a mortar and pestle to form a smooth paste.

- Trim the chicken of any fat, then chop into 2 cm (3/4 inch) pieces and put in a large bowl. Add red curry paste and mix well to coat the chicken in the paste.

- Put the chicken in the slow cooker. Cook on high for 2 hours, then add the coconut cream and cook for a further 1 hour. Ladle the curry into large serving bowls and garnish with the coriander leaves and chilli. Serve with jasmine rice.

Hot & spicy

CREAMY CHICKEN CURRY

preparation time 30 minutes +
cooking time 4 hours
serves 4

2 cm (3/4 inch) piece fresh ginger, roughly chopped

3 garlic cloves, roughly chopped

1 kg (2 lb 4 oz) boneless, skinless chicken thighs

75 g (2¹/2 oz/¹/2 cup) blanched almonds

150 g (5¹/2 oz) Greek-style yoghurt

¹/2 teaspoon chilli powder

¹/4 teaspoon ground cloves

¹/4 teaspoon ground cinnamon

1 teaspoon garam masala

4 cardamom pods, lightly crushed

400 g (14 oz) tinned chopped tomatoes

1 large onion, thinly sliced

1 handful coriander (cilantro) leaves, finely chopped

80 ml (2¹/2 fl oz/¹/3 cup) thick (double/heavy) cream

- Using a mortar and pestle or a food processor, crush or blend the ginger and garlic together to form a paste. Alternatively, finely grate the ginger and crush the garlic and mix them together.

- Trim the chicken of any excess fat and cut into fairly large pieces. Set aside while you prepare the marinade.

- Grind the almonds in a food processor or finely chop with a knife. Put the ginger, garlic paste and almonds in a large bowl with the yoghurt, chilli powder, cloves, cinnamon, garam masala, cardamom pods, tomatoes and 1 teaspoon salt. Blend together with a fork. Add chicken pieces and stir to coat the chicken thoroughly. Cover and marinate for 2 hours, or overnight, in the refrigerator.

- Combine chicken mixture with the onion in the slow cooker. Cook on high for 3 hours. Add half the coriander and the cream and cook for a further 1 hour, or until the chicken is tender.

- Season to taste with salt and freshly ground black pepper. Serve the chicken with rice and garnish with the remaining coriander.

CHICKEN BRAISED WITH GINGER AND STAR ANISE

preparation time 15 minutes
cooking time 2 hours
serves 4

1 kg (2 lb 4 oz) boneless, skinless
   chicken thighs
1 teaspoon sichuan peppercorns
3 x 2 cm (1¼ x ¾ inch) piece fresh
   ginger, shredded
2 garlic cloves, chopped
80 ml (2½ fl oz/⅓ cup) Chinese rice
   wine

60 ml (2 fl oz/¼ cup) light soy sauce
1 tablespoon honey
1 star anise
3 spring onions (scallions), thinly
   sliced diagonally

• Trim the chicken of any fat, then cut each thigh in half. Put the chicken pieces, peppercorns, ginger, garlic, rice wine, soy sauce, honey and the star anise in the slow cooker. Cook on high for 2 hours, or until the chicken is tender and cooked through.

• Season with salt and freshly ground black pepper. Garnish with the spring onions and serve with steamed rice.

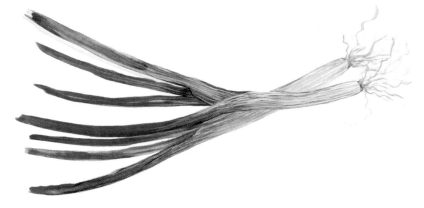

GREEN CHICKEN CURRY

preparation time 20 minutes
cooking time 2 hours
serves 4–6

750 g (1 lb 10 oz) boneless,
   skinless chicken thighs
2 tablespoons green curry paste
435 ml (15$^{1}/_{4}$ fl oz/1$^{3}/_{4}$ cups) coconut
   milk
350 g (12 oz) long, thin eggplants
   (aubergines), sliced
7 makrut (kaffir lime) leaves,
   torn in half

2$^{1}/_{2}$ tablespoons fish sauce
1 tablespoon grated palm sugar
   (jaggery) or soft brown sugar
1 handful Thai sweet basil, to garnish
1 long red chilli, seeded and thinly
   sliced, to garnish

● Trim chicken of any fat, then cut each thigh into 5 cm (2 inch) pieces.
Put chicken, curry paste, coconut milk, eggplant and four lime leaves in the
slow cooker. Cook on high for 2 hours, or until the chicken is tender.

● Stir through the fish sauce, sugar and remaining lime leaves. Garnish with
basil and chilli and serve with steamed rice.

Hot & spicy

CHICKEN AND PRUNE TAGINE

preparation time 15 minutes
cooking time 3 hours
serves 4

800 g (1 lb 12 oz) boneless, skinless
   chicken thighs
1 onion, chopped
$1/4$ teaspoon ground saffron threads
$1/2$ teaspoon ground ginger
2 cinnamon sticks
4 coriander (cilantro) sprigs, tied in
   a bunch

zest of $1/2$ lemon, removed in wide
   strips
300 g ($10^1/2$ oz/$1^1/3$ cups) pitted
   prunes
2 tablespoons honey
1 tablespoon sesame seeds, toasted

● Trim the chicken of any fat, then cut each thigh into quarters. Put the chicken pieces, onion, saffron, ginger, cinnamon sticks, bunch of coriander sprigs and 250 ml (9 fl oz/1 cup) water in the slow cooker. Cook on high for $2^1/2$ hours, or until the chicken is tender.

● Add the strips of lemon zest, prunes and honey, cover and cook for a further 30 minutes, or until the chicken is very tender and cooked through. Remove and discard the coriander sprigs. Serve hot, sprinkled with sesame seeds.

BUTTER CHICKEN

preparation time 20 minutes
cooking time 4^1/$_4$ hours
serves 6

1 kg (2 lb 4 oz) boneless, skinless
   chicken thighs
2 teaspoons garam masala
2 teaspoons sweet paprika
2 teaspoons ground coriander
1 tablespoon grated fresh ginger
^{1}/$_4$ teaspoon chilli powder
1 cinnamon stick

6 cardamom pods, bruised
375 g (13 oz/1^1/$_2$ cups) tomato
   passata (puréed tomatoes)
60 g (2^1/$_4$ oz/^{1}/$_4$ cup) plain yoghurt
2 tablespoons cornflour (cornstarch)
1 tablespoon sugar
125 ml (4 fl oz/^{1}/$_2$ cup) pouring cream
1 tablespoon lemon juice

● Trim chicken of any fat, then cut each thigh into quarters. Put chicken pieces, garam masala, paprika, coriander, ginger, chilli, cinnamon stick, cardamom and tomato passata in the slow cooker. Cook on low for 4 hours, or until the chicken is tender and cooked through.

● Combine the yoghurt with the cornflour. Turn the slow cooker heat to high. Add the yoghurt mixture to the slow cooker along with the sugar, cream and lemon juice. Cook for a further 10 minutes, or until the sauce has thickened slightly. Serve with steamed rice.

Hot & spicy

PORK VINDALOO

preparation time 25 minutes +
cooking time 3^1/$_2$ hours
serves 4

800 g (1 lb 12 oz) boneless pork leg
6 cardamom pods
1 teaspoon black peppercorns
4 dried chillies
1 teaspoon cloves
10 cm (4 inch) piece cinnamon stick,
   roughly broken
1 teaspoon cumin seeds
^{1}/$_2$ teaspoon coriander seeds
^{1}/$_4$ teaspoon fenugreek seeds
^{1}/$_2$ teaspoon ground turmeric
80 ml (2^1/$_2$ fl oz/^{1}/$_3$ cup) white wine
   vinegar

1 tablespoon balsamic vinegar
2 onions, thinly sliced
10 garlic cloves, thinly sliced
5 cm (2 inch) piece fresh ginger,
   cut into matchsticks
250 g (9 oz/1 cup) tomato passata
   (puréed tomatoes)
4 green chillies, seeded and chopped
1 teaspoon grated palm sugar
   (jaggery) or soft brown sugar

- Trim the pork leg of any excess fat and cut the meat into 2.5 cm (1 inch) cubes. Set aside while you make the marinade.

- Split open the cardamom pods and remove the seeds. Using a mortar and pestle or a spice grinder, finely pound or grind cardamom seeds, peppercorns, dried chillies, cloves, cinnamon stick, cumin seeds, coriander seeds, fenugreek seeds and turmeric.

- In a large bowl, mix the ground spices together with the vinegars. Add pork and mix thoroughly to coat well. Cover and marinate in refrigerator for 3 hours.

- Combine the pork, onion, garlic, ginger, tomato passata, chilli and sugar in the slow cooker. Cook on high for 3 1/2 hours, or until the pork is very tender. Serve with steamed rice.

PORK WITH ONION AND BARBECUE SAUCE

preparation time 20 minutes
cooking time 7 hours
serves 4–6

250 g (9 oz/1 cup) barbecue sauce
1¹/2 tablespoons roughly chopped
   jalapeño chilli
1/2 teaspoon ground cumin
1/4 teaspoon ground cinnamon
1 teaspoon paprika
45 g (1¹/2 oz/1/4 cup) soft brown sugar
2 garlic cloves, chopped
1 teaspoon dijon mustard

2 tablepoons red wine vinegar
2 teaspoons worcestershire sauce
1 onion, thinly sliced
1.6 kg (3 lb 8 oz) boned, rolled pork
   loin
1 tablespoon coriander (cilantro)
   leaves, chopped
bread rolls, to serve

● Put the barbecue sauce, jalapeño, cumin, cinnamon, paprika, brown sugar, garlic, mustard, vinegar and worcestershire sauce in a small bowl. Add 250 ml (9 fl oz/1 cup) water and stir to combine.

● Put the onion in the base of the slow cooker. Add pork and pour the sauce over the top. Cook on high for 7 hours, or until the pork is tender. When pork is cool enough to handle, shred meat apart using two forks or your fingers. Stir in the chopped coriander.

● Serve the pork topped with the onion and barbecue sauce on fresh bread rolls. Serve with a side salad if desired.

JAPANESE SLOW-COOKED PORK BELLY

preparation time 20 minutes
cooking time 5 hours
serves 4–6

1 kg (2 lb 4 oz) boneless pork belly
100 g (3¹/₂ oz) fresh ginger, cut into
    thick slices
500 ml (17 fl oz/2 cups) dashi
    (made up according to packet
    instructions)
170 ml (5¹/₂ fl oz/²/₃ cup) sake

60 ml (2 fl oz/¹/₄ cup) mirin
80 g (2³/₄ oz/¹/₃ cup firmly packed)
    dark brown sugar
125 ml (4 fl oz/¹/₂ cup) Japanese soy
    sauce
Japanese mustard, to serve (optional)

- Cut the pork into 5 cm (2 inch) cubes. Put the pork, ginger, dashi, sake, mirin, brown sugar and soy sauce in the slow cooker. Pour in 375 ml (13 fl oz/1¹/₂ cups) water. Cook on low for 4¹/₂ hours, or until the pork is tender.

- Remove the lid and increase the slow cooker heat to high. Cook for a further 30 minutes, or until the sauce is slightly reduced. Serve with Japanese mustard on the side if desired and steamed rice.

Hot & spicy

SICHUAN AND ANISE BEEF STEW

preparation time 20 minutes
cooking time 3 hours
serves 4

1 kg (2 lb 4 oz) chuck steak
1¹/₂ tablespoons plain (all-purpose)
   flour
1 large red onion, thickly sliced
2 garlic cloves, crushed
3 tablespoons tomato paste
   (concentrated purée)
250 ml (9 fl oz/1 cup) red wine
250 ml (9 fl oz/1 cup) beef stock

2 bay leaves, crushed
3 long strips orange zest
2 star anise
1 teaspoon sichuan peppercorns
1 teaspoon chopped thyme
1 tablespoon chopped rosemary
3 tablespoons chopped coriander
   (cilantro)

- Trim the beef and cut into 3 cm (1¹/₄ inch) cubes. Put the beef, flour, onion, garlic, tomato paste, wine, stock, bay leaves, strips of orange zest, star anise, peppercorns, thyme and the rosemary in the slow cooker. Cook on high heat for 3 hours, or until the beef is tender.

- Season to taste with salt and freshly ground black pepper. Stir in most of the coriander leaves and garnish with the remainder. Serve stew with steamed rice.

MUSSAMAN CURRY

preparation time 20 minutes
cooking time 4 hours
serves 4

800 g (1 lb 12 oz) chuck steak
2 cinnamon sticks
10 cardamom seeds
5 cloves
2 tablespoons mussaman curry paste
250 ml (9 fl oz/1 cup) coconut milk
2–3 all-purpose potatoes, cut into
    2.5 cm (1 inch) pieces

2 cm ($3/4$ inch) piece fresh ginger,
    shredded
60 ml (2 fl oz/$1/4$ cup) fish sauce
60 g (2 oz/$1/4$ cup) grated palm sugar
    (jaggery) or soft brown sugar
110 g ($3 3/4$ oz/$2/3$ cup) roasted salted
    peanuts
3 tablespoons tamarind purée

- Trim beef and cut into 5 cm (2 inch) cubes. Put the beef, cinnamon sticks, cardamom, cloves, curry paste, coconut milk, potato, ginger, fish sauce, sugar, three–quarters of the roasted peanuts and tamarind purée in the slow cooker. Cook on high for 4 hours, or until beef is tender and the potato is just cooked.

- Taste, then adjust the seasoning with salt and freshly ground black pepper if necessary. Spoon into serving bowls and garnish with the remaining roasted peanuts. Serve with steamed rice.

SAAG LAMB

preparation time 30 minutes +
cooking time 5 hours
serves 4

1 kg (2 lb 4 oz) boneless lamb leg or
   shoulder
1 teaspoon fenugreek seeds
1 teaspoon cumin seeds
1 teaspoon mustard seeds
2 onions, diced
2 garlic cloves, finely chopped
2 teaspoons grated fresh ginger
2 small red chillies, seeded and finely
   diced
2 cinnamon sticks

4 fresh curry leaves
250 ml (9 fl oz/1 cup) beef stock
400 g (14 oz) baby English spinach

CORIANDER YOGHURT
125 g (4^{1}/$_{2}$ oz/^{1}/$_{2}$ cup) Greek-style
   yoghurt
1 tablespoon lemon juice
1 small handful coriander (cilantro)
   leaves, chopped

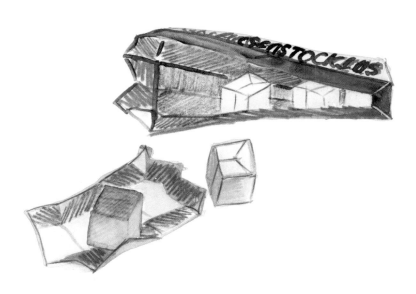

• Trim the lamb of excess fat, then cut into 3 cm (1 1/4 inch) cubes. Put the
lamb in a large bowl.

• Using a mortar and pestle or spice grinder, pound or grind the fenugreek,
cumin and mustard seeds. Combine the ground spices with the onion, garlic,
ginger and chilli. Stir the spice mixture into the lamb, stirring well to coat the
lamb with the spices. Cover and leave to marinate in the refrigerator overnight.

• Put the lamb, cinnamon sticks, curry leaves and stock in the slow cooker.
Cook on high for 4 hours, then add the spinach and cook for a further 1 hour,
or until the lamb is tender.

• Meanwhile, to make the coriander yoghurt, combine yoghurt, lemon juice
and coriander. Serve lamb with coriander yoghurt and steamed basmati rice.

LAMB KORMA

preparation time 20 minutes
cooking time 3¹/₄ hours
serves 4–6

1 kg (2 lb 4 oz) boneless lamb leg or
    shoulder
2 tablespoons Greek-style yoghurt
60 g (2¹/₄ oz/¹/₄ cup) korma paste
2 onions
2 tablespoons desiccated coconut
3 green chillies, roughly chopped
4 garlic cloves, crushed
5 cm (2 inch) piece fresh ginger,
    grated

50 g (1³/₄ oz/¹/₃ cup) cashew nuts
6 cloves
¹/₄ teaspoon ground cinnamon
125 ml (4 fl oz/¹/₂ cup) chicken stock
6 cardamom pods, crushed
2 tablespoons pouring cream
1 handful coriander (cilantro) leaves,
    to garnish

• Trim the lamb of excess fat and cut into 2.5 cm (1 inch) cubes. Put lamb in a bowl, add the yoghurt and korma paste and mix to coat the lamb thoroughly.

• Roughly chop one onion and thinly slice the other. Put the roughly chopped onion, coconut, chilli, garlic, ginger, cashew nuts, cloves and cinnamon in the bowl of a food processor. Add the stock and process to form a smooth paste. Alternatively, finely chop the ingredients with a knife before adding the stock.

• Put lamb, spice mixture, sliced onion, cardamom and a pinch of salt in the slow cooker. Cook on high for 3 hours, or until lamb is tender. Stir through the cream and cook for a further 10 minutes. Season to taste with salt and freshly ground black pepper.

• Ladle the curry into serving bowls over steamed rice and sprinkle with the coriander leaves.

AFRICAN-STYLE LAMB AND PEANUT STEW

preparation time 30 minutes
cooking time 4–6 hours
serves 4–6

1 kg (2 lb 4 oz) lamb (such as
    boneless lamb leg steaks)
3 teaspoons curry powder
1 teaspoon dried oregano
pinch cayenne pepper
1 large onion, chopped
1 large carrot, chopped
1 red capsicum (pepper), seeded
    and chopped
500 g (1 lb 2 oz) orange sweet
    potato, cut into 2 cm (3/4 inch)
    cubes
4 garlic cloves, chopped

1 red or green chilli, seeded and finely
    chopped
400 g (14 oz) tinned chopped
    tomatoes
125 ml (4 fl oz/1/2 cup) tomato sauce
    (ketchup)
2 bay leaves
90 g (31/4 oz/1/3 cup) crunchy or
    smooth peanut butter
1 tablespoon lemon juice
165 ml (51/2 fl oz) tinned coconut milk
155 g (51/2 oz/1 cup) fresh or frozen
    peas

● Trim the lamb of any fat and cut into 2 cm (3/4 inch) cubes. Put lamb in a large bowl and sprinkle over the curry powder, oregano and cayenne pepper. Season with salt and freshly ground black pepper. Toss well to coat the lamb.

● Add onion, carrot, capsicum, sweet potato, garlic, chilli, tomatoes, tomato sauce and bay leaves to the lamb. Toss to thoroughly combine all ingredients. Transfer lamb and vegetables to slow cooker. Cook on high for 4–6 hours, or until the lamb and vegetables are tender and cooked through.

● Meanwhile, combine peanut butter, lemon juice and coconut milk in a small bowl. During the last 30 minutes of cooking, add the peanut butter mixture to the slow cooker and stir to combine the ingredients. Add the peas and cook for 5 minutes, or until tender.

● Remove the bay leaves and discard. Divide the stew among bowls and serve with steamed rice or couscous.

ROGAN JOSH

preparation time 20 minutes +
cooking time 6 hours
serves 6

1 kg (2 lb 4 oz) boneless lamb leg or
   shoulder
3 garlic cloves, crushed
6 cm (2¹/₂ inch) piece fresh ginger,
   grated
2 teaspoons ground cumin
1 teaspoon chilli powder
2 teaspoons paprika
2 teaspoons ground coriander
1 onion, finely chopped

6 cardamom pods, crushed
4 cloves
2 bay leaves
1 cinnamon stick
200 g (7 oz) plain yoghurt
4 saffron threads
2 tablespoons milk
¹/₂ teaspoon garam masala
coriander (cilantro) sprigs, to garnish

- Trim the lamb of excess fat and then cut it into 4 cm (1 1/2 inch) cubes.

- Mix together garlic, ginger, cumin, chilli powder, paprika and ground coriander in a large bowl. Add the lamb and stir thoroughly to coat the lamb in the spices. Cover and then marinate in the refrigerator for at least 2 hours, or overnight.

- Put lamb mixture in the slow cooker. Stir in the onion, cardamom, cloves, bay leaves, cinnamon stick, yoghurt and 60 ml (2 fl oz/1/4 cup) water. Cook on low for 6 hours, or until the lamb is tender.

- Meanwhile, combine the saffron with the milk and then set aside to soak for 10 minutes. Just before the end of cooking time, stir saffron and milk mixture, along with the garam masala, into the lamb in the slow cooker. Season to taste with salt. Serve the curry with steamed rice and garnish with coriander sprigs.

MOROCCAN SPICED LAMB WITH PUMPKIN

preparation time 20 minutes
cooking time 5 hours
serves 6

1.5 kg (3 lb 5 oz) boneless lamb
   shoulder
1 large onion, diced
1 teaspoon ground coriander
$1/2$ teaspoon ground ginger
$1/2$ teaspoon cayenne pepper
$1/4$ teaspoon ground saffron threads
1 cinnamon stick

500 ml (17 fl oz/2 cups) chicken stock
500 g (1 lb 2 oz) pumpkin (winter
   squash), cut into 2 cm ($3/4$ inch)
   dice
100 g ($3^1/2$ oz) dried apricots
coriander (cilantro) sprigs, to garnish

• Trim the lamb of excess fat and cut into 3 cm (1$1/4$ inch) cubes. Put lamb, onion, ground coriander, ginger, cayenne pepper, saffron, cinnamon stick, stock and pumpkin in slow cooker. Cook on low for 4 hours. Add apricots and cook for a further 1 hour.

• Taste the sauce and adjust the seasoning with salt and freshly ground black pepper if necessary. Transfer to a warm serving dish and garnish with coriander sprigs. Serve with couscous or rice.

LAMB SHANKS WITH TOMATO, CHILLI AND HONEY

preparation time 15 minutes
cooking time 8 hours
serves 4

8 lamb shanks, French trimmed
2 garlic cloves, thinly sliced
1 large onion, sliced
250 ml (9 fl oz/1 cup) red wine
2 teaspoons dried oregano
1/2 teaspoon chilli flakes

500 g (1 lb 2 oz/2 cups) tomato
   passata (puréed tomatoes)
250 ml (9 fl oz/1 cup) chicken stock
90 g (3 1/4 oz/1/4 cup) honey
1 tablespoon chopped flat-leaf
   (Italian) parsley

• Put lamb shanks, garlic, onion, wine, oregano, chilli flakes, tomato passata, stock and honey in the slow cooker. Cook on low for 8 hours, or until shanks are tender.

• Stir through parsley and season with salt and freshly ground black pepper. Serve with steamed rice.

Pulses & grains

For inexpensive, nutritious meals, choose pulses and grains. They are ideal ingredients for the slow-cooking process.

BOSTON-STYLE BAKED BEANS WITH HAM

preparation time 20 minutes +
cooking time 8–10 hours
serves 6

400 g (14 oz/2 cups) dried cannellini
 beans
1 large onion, finely chopped
1.5 kg (3 lb 5 oz) ham hock
1 bay leaf
60 ml (2 fl oz/^{1}/$_4$ cup) molasses
80 g (2^3/$_4$ oz/^{1}/$_3$ cup firmly packed)
 soft brown sugar

160 g (5^1/$_2$ oz/^{2}/$_3$ cup) tomato paste
 (concentrated purée)
2 tablespoons worcestershire sauce
1 teaspoon mustard powder
1 garlic clove

● Soak the beans in a large saucepan of water overnight. Drain, discarding the water, then put the beans in a saucepan with fresh water, bring to the boil and boil rapidly for 10 minutes. Rinse and drain again.

● Put beans, onion, ham hock, bay leaf, molasses, brown sugar, tomato paste, worcestershire sauce, mustard, garlic and 750 ml (26 fl oz/3 cups) water in the slow cooker. Cook on low for 8–10 hours, or until the beans are soft.

● Carefully remove the hock. When cool enough to handle, cut the meat from the bone. Pull meat apart or cut it into smallish chunks, then return to the slow cooker and stir to combine well. Cook, uncovered, for a further 30 minutes, or until sauce is thick and syrupy. Serve the baked beans with thick buttered toast or cornbread to mop up the juices.

KEDGEREE

preparation time 15 minutes
cooking time 3 hours
serves 4

500 g (1 lb 2 oz/2¹/2 cups)
   par-cooked long-grain rice
1 onion, finely chopped
2 tablespoons mild Indian curry paste
1 teaspoon ground cumin
2 bay leaves
500 ml (17 fl oz/2 cups) chicken or
   fish stock
500 g (1 lb 2 oz) boneless, skinless
   salmon fillets

125 ml (4 fl oz/¹/2 cup) pouring cream
50 g (1³/4 oz) butter
155 g (5¹/2 oz/1 cup) fresh or frozen
   peas
2 tablespoons chopped parsley
2 tablespoons lemon juice

● Put rice, onion, curry paste, cumin and bay leaves in the slow cooker. Pour over stock and 250 ml (9 fl oz/1 cup) water. Cook on low for 2¹/2 hours, or until the rice is almost tender.

● Meanwhile, prepare the salmon. Check for any bones and remove with your fingers or tweezers. Cut the salmon into 3 cm (1¹/4 inch) cubes.

● Put salmon on top of the rice, add the cream, butter and peas and cook for a further 30 minutes, or until rice is tender and the fish is cooked. Stir through parsley and lemon juice and season with salt and freshly ground black pepper.

MILD CURRY OF CHICKEN, SWEET POTATOES AND SPLIT PEAS

preparation time 20 minutes +
cooking time 3–4 hours
serves 4–6

220 g (7³/4 oz/1 cup) dried yellow
   split peas
2 boneless, skinless chicken breasts
1 tablespoon vegetable oil
1 red onion, chopped
2 garlic cloves, crushed
1 tablespoon grated fresh ginger
3 teaspoons curry powder
500 g (1 lb 2 oz) orange sweet
   potato, cut into 2 cm (³/4 inch)
   cubes

100 g (3¹/2 oz) green beans, trimmed
   and cut into 4 cm (1¹/2 inch)
   lengths
400 g (14 oz) tinned chopped
   tomatoes
250 ml (9 fl oz/1 cup) chicken stock
125 ml (4 fl oz/¹/2 cup) pouring cream
1 small handful coriander (cilantro)
   leaves, chopped

• Put the split peas in a bowl, cover with plenty of water and soak for several hours or overnight. Drain.

• Trim the chicken of any fat and cut into 2 cm (^{3}/4 inch) cubes.

• Pour oil into the slow cooker bowl and spread over the base and side. Add onion, garlic and ginger and stir in the curry powder. Add split peas, chicken, sweet potato and beans. Pour over the tomatoes and stock and season well with salt and freshly ground black pepper.

• Cook on high for 3–4 hours, or until split peas and sweet potato are cooked. Stir occasionally during cooking time. Just before serving, stir in the cream and coriander and heat through for a few minutes. Serve with basmati rice.

BROWN RICE AND BARLEY RISOTTO WITH PUMPKIN AND CHICKEN

preparation time 20 minutes +
cooking time 3–3¹/₂ hours
serves 4

330 g (11¹/₂ oz/1¹/₂ cups) short-grain
  brown rice
110 g (3³/₄ oz/¹/₂ cup) pearl barley
1 boneless, skinless chicken breast
1 tablespoon olive oil
1 red onion, finely chopped
350 g (12 oz) pumpkin (winter
  squash), peeled, seeded and cut
  into1 cm (¹/₂ inch) dice
12 sage leaves

1 teaspoon vegetable or chicken
  stock powder (optional)
60 ml (2 fl oz/¹/₄ cup) white wine
155 g (5¹/₂ oz/1 cup) fresh or frozen
  peas
50 g (1³/₄ oz/¹/₂ cup) freshly grated
  parmesan cheese, plus extra,
  to serve
sage leaves, to serve (optional)

- Put the rice and barley in a bowl and cover with 1 litre (35 fl oz/4 cups) water. Leave to soak for 8 hours, or overnight.

- Trim the chicken of excess fat and cut into bite-sized cubes. Pour the olive oil into the slow cooker bowl and spread the oil over the base and side. Pour rice and barley, along with the soaking water, into the slow cooker. Add the chicken, onion, pumpkin and sage. Mix the stock powder, if using, with the wine, then stir it into the grains. Season well with salt and freshly ground black pepper.

- Cook on high for 3 hours, or until all liquid has been absorbed and the rice and barley are tender. Stir occasionally during cooking time. If grains are not quite cooked after 3 hours, cook for a further 20–30 minutes, or until tender.

- Before serving, beat the grains with a fork to thoroughly mix in the cooked pumpkin until it looks 'creamy'. Stir in the peas and the parmesan and cook for a further 5 minutes, or until the peas are cooked through.

- Season to taste with salt and freshly ground black pepper. Spoon into serving bowls and top with extra grated parmesan cheese and sage leaves if desired.

Note   *Leave out the chicken and chicken stock for a vegetarian version.*

ARROZ CON POLLO

preparation time 20 minutes
cooking time 9 hours
serves 6

4 very ripe tomatoes
2 kg (4 lb 8 oz) chicken pieces, skin
   removed
100 g (3¹/₂ oz) chorizo sausage,
   sliced
1 large onion, finely chopped
1 green capsicum (pepper), seeded
   and diced
1 tablespoon sweet paprika
1 long red chilli, seeded and finely
   chopped
2 garlic cloves, crushed

pinch saffron threads (optional)
250 ml (9 fl oz/1 cup) chicken stock
2¹/₂ tablespoons tomato paste
   (concentrated purée)
80 ml (2¹/₂ fl oz/¹/₃ cup) sherry
400 g (14 oz/2 cups) par-cooked rice
100 g (3¹/₂ oz/²/₃ cup) frozen peas
3 tablespoons finely chopped flat-leaf
   (Italian) parsley
55 g (2 oz/¹/₃ cup) stuffed green
   olives (optional)

- Score a cross in the base of each tomato. Put tomatoes in a heatproof bowl and cover with boiling water. Leave for 30 seconds, then transfer to cold water, drain and peel the skin away from the cross. Cut the tomatoes in half, scoop out the seeds with a teaspoon and roughly chop the flesh.

- Put tomato, chicken pieces, chorizo, onion, capsicum, paprika, chilli, garlic, saffron (if using), stock, tomato paste and sherry in the slow cooker. Cook on low for 8 hours.

- Add rice to the slow cooker and stir to coat well. Cook for a further 1 hour, or until the liquid has absorbed, then stir in the peas, cover and cook for a further 5 minutes, or until the rice, peas and chicken are tender and cooked through.

- Stir in the parsley and olives, if using, and season to taste with salt and freshly ground black pepper. Serve immediately.

JAMBALAYA

preparation time 30 minutes
cooking time 3 hours
serves 4

4 vine-ripened tomatoes
1/2 teaspoon saffron threads
1 red onion, sliced
3 bacon slices, rind and fat removed,
    chopped
2 chorizo sausages, cut into 1 cm
    (1/2 inch) slices diagonally
1 small red capsicum (pepper),
    seeded and sliced
1 small green capsicum (pepper),
    seeded and sliced

2 garlic cloves, finely chopped
1–2 teaspoons seeded, finely
    chopped jalapeño chilli
1 teaspoon smoked paprika
3 teaspoons Cajun spice mix
400 g (14 oz/2 cups) par-cooked
    long-grain rice, rinsed
250 ml (9 fl oz/1 cup) beer
500 ml (17 fl oz/2 cups) chicken stock
2 boneless, skinless chicken breasts
16 raw prawns (shrimp)

- Score a cross in the base of each tomato. Put tomatoes in a heatproof bowl and cover with boiling water. Leave for 30 seconds, then transfer to cold water, drain and peel skin away from cross. Cut tomatoes into quarters and set aside.

- Put the saffron in a small bowl with 1 tablespoon warm water and set aside for 10 minutes to soak.

- Put the onion, bacon, chorizo, red and green capsicum, garlic, chilli, paprika, Cajun spice mix, rice, beer and stock in slow cooker. Add the tomato quarters and the saffron and its soaking liquid. Cook on low for 2 hours, or until the rice is tender and the stock is absorbed.

- Meanwhile, prepare the chicken and prawns. Trim the chicken of any fat and cut into 1.5 x 6 cm (5/8 x 21/2 inch) strips. Peel prawns, leaving the tails intact. Gently pull out the dark vein from each prawn back, starting at the head end.

- Add chicken and prawns to the slow cooker, stir to combine the ingredients, and cook for a further 1 hour, or until the chicken and prawns are cooked.

PORK BELLY WITH VEGETABLES AND LENTILS

preparation time 20 minutes
cooking time 5 hours
serves 6

1 kg (2 lb 4 oz) pork belly
1 onion
4 cloves
1 large carrot, cut into chunks
200 g (7 oz) swede (rutabaga) or
   turnips, cut into chunks
100 g (3½ oz) leek, white part only,
   thickly sliced
1 parsnip, cut into chunks

1 garlic clove
1 bouquet garni
2 bay leaves
6 juniper berries, slightly crushed
350 g (12 oz/1¾ cups) puy lentils or
   tiny blue-green lentils
2 tablespoons chopped flat-leaf
   (Italian) parsley

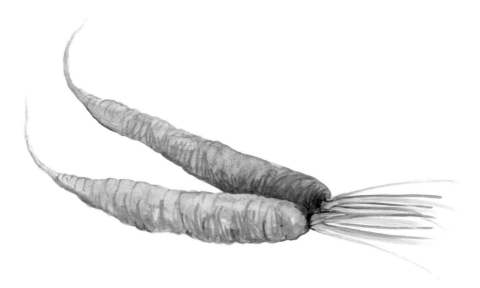

• Slice the pork belly into thick strips. Stud the onion with the cloves. Put the pork strips in the slow cooker along with the studded onion and all remaining ingredients except for the lentils and parsley. Stir thoroughly, then add just enough water to half cover the ingredients. Cook on high for 4 hours.

• Put the lentils in a sieve and rinse under cold running water. Add to the slow cooker and cook for a further 1 hour, or until pork and lentils are tender and cooked through.

• Drain mixture into a colander, discarding the liquid. Return the contents of the colander to the slow cooker, except for the onion, which can be discarded.

• Season the pork and lentils with plenty of freshly ground black pepper and taste to see if you need any salt. Just before serving, stir in the chopped parsley.

CASSOULET

preparation time 20 minutes
cooking time 6–8 hours
serves 4

4 pork spare ribs (600 g/1 lb 5 oz)
4 thick beef or lamb sausages
6 French shallots, peeled and
   chopped
1 carrot, diced
1 celery stalk, diced
3–4 garlic cloves, chopped
$1/2$ teaspoon paprika
1 large rosemary sprig or 1 teaspoon
   dried rosemary

2 tablespoons tomato paste
   (concentrated purée)
400 g (14 oz) tinned chopped
   tomatoes
60 ml (2 fl oz/$1/4$ cup) white wine
800 g (1 lb 12 oz) tinned white
   beans, such as cannellini, haricot or
   butter beans, drained and rinsed
1 small handful flat-leaf (Italian)
   parsley, chopped

• Prepare the spare ribs by removing the rind and excess fat. Cut each spare rib into three thick chunks. Cut the sausages in half.

• Put the ribs, sausages, shallots, carrot, celery and garlic in the slow cooker. Sprinkle over the paprika and tuck in the rosemary sprig (or sprinkle over the dried rosemary). Season with salt and freshly ground black pepper.

• Combine the tomato paste with the tomatoes and wine and pour over the meat and vegetables. Stir in the beans.

• Cook on low for 6–8 hours, or until the meat is tender. Remove the rosemary sprig and stir through the parsley. Serve the cassoulet with crusty bread.

CHILLI BEEF WITH CAPSICUM, CORIANDER AND AVOCADO

preparation time 30 minutes
cooking time 6 hours
serves 6

800 g (1 lb 12 oz) chuck steak
800 g (1 lb 12 oz) tinned chopped
  tomatoes
1 red capsicum (pepper), seeded and
  diced
110 g (3³/₄ oz) dark-gilled field
  mushrooms, finely chopped
2 onions, chopped
2 garlic cloves, crushed
4 medium–hot green chillies, seeded
  and finely chopped
2 teaspoons ground cumin
¹/₂ teaspoon ground cinnamon

1 teaspoon caster (superfine) sugar
2 bay leaves
200 ml (7 fl oz) beef stock
1 large handful coriander (cilantro)
  leaves
400 g (14 oz) tinned red kidney
  beans, drained and rinsed
25 g (1 oz) dark, bitter chocolate
  (Mexican if possible), grated
1 firm, ripe avocado
¹/₂ red onion, chopped
250 g (9 oz/1 cup) sour cream

- Trim the beef of excess fat and cut into cubes. Put the beef, tomatoes, capsicum, mushrooms, onion, garlic, chilli, cumin, cinnamon, sugar and bay leaves in the slow cooker. Pour the stock over the beef and vegetables and cook on low for 6 hours, or until the beef is tender.

- Stir in half the coriander, kidney beans and chocolate. Season with salt and extra chopped chilli if desired. Cook for a further 5 minutes, or until the beans are warmed through.

- Chop avocado and mix with red onion and remaining coriander leaves. Top each serving of chilli beef with a spoonful of sour cream and a spoonful of the avocado mixture.

TURKISH MEATBALLS WITH RICE

preparation time 30 minutes
cooking time 4 hours
serves 4–6

500 g (1 lb 2 oz) minced (ground)
  beef
1/2 teaspoon allspice
1 teaspoon ground cinnamon
2 teaspoons ground cumin
1 teaspoon ground coriander
330 g (11 1/2 oz/1 1/2 cups) par-cooked
  short-grain rice
375 ml (13 fl oz/1 1/2 cups) chicken
  stock

400 g (14 oz) tinned chopped
  tomatoes
35 g (1 1/4 oz/ 1/4 cup) toasted
  pistachio nuts
2 tablespoons currants
2 tablespoons chopped coriander
  (cilantro) leaves

• Put beef in a bowl and add allspice, 1/2 teaspoon of cinnamon, 1 teaspoon of cumin and 1/2 teaspoon of coriander. Season with salt and freshly ground black pepper. Using your hands, mix the spices and the beef together well, and then roll the mixture into small balls.

• Put meatballs in the slow cooker along with the remaining spices, rice, stock and tomatoes. Cook on high for 4 hours, or until meatballs and rice are cooked through. Stir through pistachios, currants and coriander before serving.

ROSEMARY–INFUSED LAMB AND LENTIL CASSEROLE

preparation time 20 minutes
cooking time 5 hours
serves 6

1 kg (2 lb 4 oz) boned lamb leg
1 onion, thinly sliced
2 garlic cloves, crushed
1 small carrot, finely chopped
2 teaspoons finely chopped fresh
  ginger
2 teaspoons rosemary leaves

500 ml (17 fl oz/2 cups) lamb or
  chicken stock
185 g (6^1/$_2$ oz/1 cup) green or brown
  lentils
1 tablespoon soft brown sugar
2 teaspoons balsamic vinegar
rosemary sprigs, to garnish

● Trim lamb of excess fat and cut into 4 cm (1^1/$_2$ inch) cubes. Put lamb, onion, garlic, carrot, ginger, rosemary, stock and lentils in slow cooker. Cook on high for 4 hours.

● Stir through brown sugar and vinegar and cook for a further 1 hour, or until the lentils are cooked and lamb is tender. Season to taste with salt and freshly ground black pepper, and garnish with rosemary sprigs.

Pulses & grains

SPICED LAMB WITH RED LENTILS

preparation time 30 minutes

cooking time 4–6 hours

serves 4

SPICE MIX

2 teaspoons ground cumin

1 teaspoon ground coriander

1/2 teaspoon ground turmeric

pinch chilli flakes

750 g (1 lb 10 oz) boneless lamb leg
   or shoulder

1 large onion, diced

1 carrot, diced

2 celery stalks, including a few leaves,
   diced

125 g (4 1/2 oz) green beans,
   trimmed and cut into 4 cm
   (1 1/2 inch) lengths

1 tablespoon grated fresh ginger

2 garlic cloves, chopped

500 ml (17 fl oz/2 cups) beef stock
   or water

250 g (9 oz/1 cup) tomato passata
   (puréed tomatoes) or tomato pasta
   sauce

1 tablespoon lemon juice

200 g (7 oz/1 cup) red lentils

1 small handful coriander (cilantro)
   leaves

- To make the spice mix, combine the ground cumin, coriander, turmeric and chilli flakes in a large bowl.

- Trim the lamb of excess fat and cut into 2 cm (3/4 inch) cubes. Add the lamb to the spice mix and toss well to thoroughly coat in the spices. Add the onion, carrot, celery and celery leaves, beans, ginger and garlic and stir to combine.

- Transfer lamb and vegetables to the slow cooker and stir in the stock, tomato passata, lemon juice and lentils. Season well with salt and freshly ground black pepper. Cook on high for 4–6 hours, or until lamb is very tender and the lentils are cooked. The mixture will become thicker the longer it is cooked, so add a little extra stock or water if necessary. Taste and then season again with salt and freshly ground black pepper.

- To serve, pile onto plates and garnish with coriander leaves and serve with basmati rice or warmed flat bread.

LAMB SHANKS WITH BARLEY AND ROOT VEGETABLES

preparation time 30 minutes +
cooking time 8–10 hours
serves 4

165 g (5¾ oz/¾ cup) pearl barley
1 onion, chopped
3 garlic cloves, crushed
1 large carrot, cut into 4 cm
   (1½ inch) pieces
1 large parsnip, cut into 4 cm
   (1½ inch) pieces
1 swede (rutabaga) or turnip, cut into
   4 cm (1½ inch) pieces
4 Frenched lamb shanks (about
   1.2 kg/2 lb 10 oz), trimmed of
   all fat (see Note)

1 teaspoon dried oregano
800 g (1 lb 12 oz) tinned chopped
   tomatoes
2 tablespoons tomato paste
   (concentrated purée)
125 ml (4 fl oz/½ cup) white wine
   or water
1 rosemary sprig
small rosemary sprigs, extra,
   to garnish

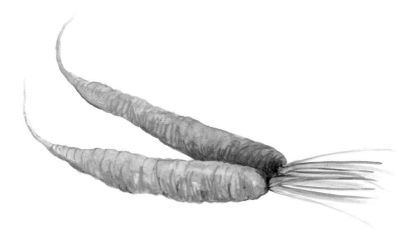

• Put the barley in a bowl and add plenty of water to cover. Soak for 8 hours, or overnight, then drain and place in the base of the slow cooker.

• Put onion, garlic, carrot, parsnip and swede on top of the barley. Top with the lamb shanks, arranged in one layer. Sprinkle over oregano and pour over the combined tomatoes, tomato paste and wine. Tuck in the rosemary sprig. Season well with salt and freshly ground black pepper.

• Cook on low for 8–10 hours, or until the lamb and barley are tender. Remove the rosemary. Skim off any surface fat.

• To serve, remove lamb shanks to a side plate. Spoon barley and vegetable mixture into wide serving bowls, top each with a shank and garnish with a small rosemary sprig.

Note   You need to use Frenched lamb shanks so they fit snugly into the slow cooker in one layer.

PERSIAN LAMB WITH CHICKPEAS

preparation time 30 minutes
cooking time 4–6 hours
serves 4–6

750 g (1 lb 10 oz) boneless lamb leg
    or shoulder 1 teaspoon ground
    cinnamon
1 teaspoon allspice
1 teaspoon freshly grated nutmeg
1 large onion, chopped
2 garlic cloves, chopped
200 g (7 oz) eggplant (aubergine), cut
    into 2 cm (3/4 inch) dice
1 carrot, chopped
1 zucchini (courgette), chopped

400 g (14 oz) tinned chopped
    tomatoes
60 ml (2 fl oz/1/4 cup) lemon juice
1 tablespoon tomato paste
    (concentrated purée)
400 g (14 oz) tinned chickpeas,
    drained and rinsed
90 g (31/4 oz/3/4 cup) raisins
60 g (21/4 oz/1/2 cup) slivered
    almonds, toasted
1 small handful mint, to garnish

- Trim the lamb of excess fat and cut into 2 cm (3/4 inch) cubes. Put the lamb in the slow cooker, sprinkle over the cinnamon, allspice and nutmeg and season with 1 teaspoon salt and some freshly ground black pepper. Stir to combine. Stir in the onion, garlic, eggplant, carrot and zucchini.

- Pour in tomatoes and lemon juice and add the tomato paste. Add chickpeas and raisins and stir well. Cook for 4–6 hours, or until the lamb is very tender.

- To serve, spoon into serving bowls and scatter over almonds and mint leaves. Serve with basmati rice and plain yoghurt if desired.

Note   *Replace the chickpeas with 400 g (14 oz) tinned red kidney beans if preferred.*

LAMB WITH WHITE BEANS

preparation time 15 minutes
cooking time 4$^{1}/_{4}$ hours
serves 4

1 kg (2 lb 4 oz) boned lamb shoulder
2 carrots, diced
2 large onions, chopped
2 garlic cloves, unpeeled
1 bouquet garni

125 ml (4 fl oz/$^{1}/_{2}$ cup) dry red wine
125 ml (4 fl oz/$^{1}/_{2}$ cup) chicken stock
400 g (14 oz) tinned cannellini beans,
    drained and rinsed

- Tie the lamb with kitchen string to keep its shape. Rub the lamb all over with salt and freshly ground black pepper.

- Put the lamb, carrot, onion, garlic, bouquet garni, wine and stock in the slow cooker. Cook on high for 4 hours, or until the lamb is tender.

- Lift lamb out of the slow cooker, cover and leave to rest for 10 minutes. Discard the bouquet garni. Skim the excess fat from the surface of the liquid in the slow cooker, then add beans. Cook, uncovered, for a further 10–15 minutes, or until beans are heated through and the sauce has thickened slightly. Season to taste with salt and freshly ground black pepper.

- Carve lamb and arrange on a platter. Spoon beans around lamb and drizzle with the sauce. Serve the remaining sauce separately.

HARIRA

preparation time 25 minutes
cooking time 5¹/₂ hours
serves 6

500 g (1 lb 2 oz) boneless lamb
   shoulder steaks
1 onion, chopped
2 garlic cloves, crushed
1¹/₂ teaspoons ground cumin
2 teaspoons paprika
¹/₂ teaspoon ground cloves
1 bay leaf
750 ml (26 fl oz/3 cups) chicken stock

500 g (1 lb 2 oz/2 cups) tomato
   passata (puréed tomatoes)
600 g (1 lb 5 oz) tinned chickpeas,
   drained and rinsed
200 g (7 oz/1 cup) par-cooked
   long-grain rice
2 large handfuls coriander (cilantro)
   leaves, chopped

● Trim the lamb of excess fat and cut into bite-sized cubes. Combine the lamb, onion, garlic, cumin, paprika, cloves, bay leaf, stock, 500 ml (17 fl oz/ 2 cups) water and the tomato passata in the slow cooker. Cook on low for 5 hours, or until the lamb is tender.

● Add the chickpeas and rice and cook for a further 30 minutes, or until the rice is tender. Stir through the coriander and serve.

Pulses & grains

LAMB BIRYANI

preparation time 25 minutes +
cooking time 7 hours
serves 6

1 kg (2 lb 4 oz) boneless lamb leg or
    shoulder
8 cm (3¹/₄ inch) piece fresh ginger,
    grated
2 garlic cloves, crushed
2 tablespoons garam masala
¹/₂ teaspoon chilli powder
¹/₂ teaspoon ground turmeric
2 green chillies, finely chopped
250 g (9 oz/1 cup) Greek-style
    yoghurt

2 onions, thinly sliced
¹/₂ teaspoon saffron threads
2 tablespoons hot milk
400 g (14 oz/2 cups) par-cooked
    basmati rice
40 g (1¹/₂ oz) butter
1 handful coriander (cilantro) leaves,
    chopped (optional)

- Trim the lamb of excess fat and cut into 3 cm (1 inch) cubes. Put the lamb in a bowl with the ginger, garlic, garam masala, chilli powder, turmeric, chilli and yoghurt. Combine well to coat the lamb in the marinade. Cover and marinate in the refrigerator overnight.

- Put lamb and marinade in the slow cooker along with onion and 1/4 teaspoon salt. Cook on low for 6 hours, or until the lamb is tender.

- Put saffron in a bowl with the hot milk and set aside for 10 minutes to soak.

- Spread rice evenly over the lamb in the slow cooker. Dot rice with the butter and drizzle with the saffron and milk. Cook for a further 1 hour, or until the rice is tender. Garnish with coriander if desired and serve immediately.

Index

Index

Index

191